The Half-Empty Heart

Also by Alan Downs, Ph.D.

Why Does This Keep Happening to Me?

The Fearless Executive

Seven Miracles of Management

Beyond the Looking Glass

Corporate Executions

The Half-Empty Heart

A SUPPORTIVE GUIDE TO BREAKING FREE

FROM CHRONIC DISCONTENT

Alan Downs, Ph.D.

ST. MARTIN'S PRESS

NEW YORK

www.stmartins.com

Library of Congress Cataloging-in-Publication Data

Downs, Alan.
    The half-empty heart : a supportive guide to breaking free from chronic discontent / Alan Downs.—1st ed.
        p. cm.
    Includes bibliographical references.
    ISBN 0-312-30795-0
    1. Depression, Mental—Treatment. I. Title.

RC537 .D695 2003
616.85'2706—dc21

                                                                2002031877

First Edition: January 2003

10 9 8 7 6 5 4 3 2 1

Contents

CONTENTS

ACKNOWLEDGMENTS

The Staff and Clients of New Moon Lodge
The Staff and Clients of "Two Worlds" Project
Karen Cote, LMSW
Don & Eunice Downs
Martha Finney
Claude Harris
Jim Kavanaugh, Ph.D.
George Kelly & Personal Construct Theory
Marian Lizzi
Donna McCoy, LPC
Dale Montieth
Nesha Morse, Ph.D.
Jennifer Neil, LISW
David Naylor
Susan Schulman
Annette Simmons
Steve Sugarman
Don & Berta Sugarman

PREFACE:

Dysthymia Is the Disease
of Chronic Discontent

This book is written for the millions of us who have suffered in silence with chronic discontent. Because we function in our jobs, communities and families, and we aren't in need of crisis intervention, we don't seek help for ourselves. We are the walking wounded and our struggle with life is sometimes called "existential anxiety" and more recently, "chronic depression." The technical term for our condition is *dysthymia*.

Even though at times we felt like it, we didn't go to bed and stay there. We pulled ourselves up in the morning and took care of our responsibilities. Although we keep pushing forward, nothing really satisfies us for long, and we struggle to feel some occasional happiness. It's like we're living in a gray fog that dulls the pleasure of our every experience. No matter what we try, whether relationships, careers, trips, or hobbies—given enough time—everything eventually leaves us feeling unsatisfied and unfulfilled.

Dysthymia is a rarely mentioned diagnostic category, yet all the research indicates that it is widespread and perhaps the most common of all psychological dysfunctions. Research shows that it affects anywhere from 6–10% of the population.

So why isn't more said about dysthymia? The answer is complex, but essentially comes down to two issues: First, historically psychotherapists have had their attentions consumed by the more severe and troubling psychological disorders. Because these disorders can be extremely debilitating, painful and even life-threatening, most of the available professional resources are focused on helping the more severely disturbed. Secondly, because dysthymia is a persistent and chronic condition (meaning lasting over a long period), it hasn't responded well to traditional therapies. Because dysthymia develops over many years and becomes deeply ingrained in the client's personality, and it takes a great deal of time and skill to address.

The truth is that mental health professionals haven't known what to do with dysthymia. Over the past 30 years, dysthymia has been reclassified from a personality disorder (something that is part of a person's personality and is relatively difficult to treat with psychotherapy) to a mood disorder (something that affects the way a person feels and traditionally has responded positively to psychotherapy and psychopharmacology) in subsequent versions of the DSM, the diagnostic manual used by all mental health professionals. Is dysthymia a character flaw or a persistent "sour mood"? This is the essence of the question professional have wrestled for nearly 50 years.

When dysthymia is discussed, it is most often dealt with as simply a milder form of major depression. This assumes (and I believe wrongly) that the most effective treatment for dysthymia is similar to that of more severe and debilitating depression.

Because of the professional muddling of dysthymia and depression, and because depression is now so well known a disease with very recognizable symptoms, I have chosen not to use the term "dysthymia" in this book. Instead, I have opted for the term *chronic discontent*, which I believe is a more descriptive and approachable term for those of us who suffer from dysthymia. Furthermore, it helps to distinguish the underlying syndrome of dysthymia from depression. (At the end of this book, I include a chapter for mental health professionals that discusses in more depth the differences between depression and dysthymia, and why it is more effective in a clinic setting to view them as different diagnosis with different treatment strategies.)

For those of us who have suffered with dysthymia, it is a real and devastating disease, and it can often develop into a more severe psychopathology if left untreated. Unlike more aggressive and debilitating disorders, dysthymia creeps slowly and only gradually disables its victims. Nonetheless, it invades every aspect of your life, diminishing its quality dramatically over time.

This book is not for everyone. If you find yourself feeling persistently hopeless, suicidal, thinking about hurting yourself or others, are dependent on alcohol or drugs, are being physically harmed by someone else or yourself, or find your body weight has changed dramatically (more than 5%), you may be suffering from something other than just dysthymia. Before going further, it is strongly recommended that you seek the help of mental health professional.

This book is written in three distinct sections. The first section is written as a discussion of dysthymia. It is intended to help you understand and recognize the disease for what it is. The second section will help you identify certain key aspects of chronic discontent in your life. Each chapter in this section deals with a specific aspect of chronic discontent and begins with a short quiz to help you discover the ways chronic discontent is affecting your life. The final section is a 5-week program that will guide you through the process of relearning the missing emotional skills and overcoming chronic discontent.

The structured program must be adhered to in its entirety if you are to achieve positive results by using it. The program is extraordinarily effective, and will challenge you, but you must adhere to the structure. All too often, readers of self-help (myself included) skip over the exercises included by the author and are content to gain a mental *appreciation* of the material rather than the *experience* of the material. Change, particularly in connection with dysthymia, only comes from experiencing the material. If you are not willing to commit to the program, you won't get the full value to be gained from this book. Life without dysthymia is very different and wonderful. The choice is yours.

Finally, I would encourage anyone who truly wants to overcome the effects of dysthymia to work through this book in conjunction with a professional psychotherapist who understands and treats dysthymia. Oftentimes the progress you make on your own will be greatly augmented by the guidance of a psychotherapist.

It is with a great joy and sense of hope for your life that I've written this book. I know life can be so much better for those who have struggled with dysthymia as I did, and as many of my patients have. The ideas in this book will change your life forever if you let them. Aren't you ready for a lasting change?

PART I

When Normal Is Below Par

1

Why Does the Happiness Never

Seem to Last?

You took the job. It felt good. But that was six months ago, and now it feels like the same old humdrum.

You married your sweetheart, and you thought life couldn't get any better. Now, you're not sure what you feel—or even if you want to be married.

You worked nights to get your nursing degree—it took you almost 8 years to do it, but you graduated with honors. Now, after a few years on the job, nursing isn't what you thought it would be. What now?

You built your dream house and included in it everything you've ever dreamed of having in a home. Now, a year later, you're thinking about selling it.

You find yourself weary with the humdrum of everyday life and often feel apathetic about things that you know should mean more to you. You try to spice up your life with new experiences, but you always seem to be in the same endless cycle of frustration and disappointment.

"What is wrong with me?" you ask yourself. "Why can't I be happy with my life? Why am I frustrated and disappointed with the way things have turned out?"

If this is you, you're not crazy. Chances are, you're struggling with a psychological condition that blocks you from feeling satisfaction and lasting happiness in your life. The condition is chronic discontent, and it is more common than you think.

Chronic discontent is one of our society's most widespread and devastating psychological disabilities. It is a slow and persistent condition that may exist for years, all the while eating away at your quality of life without causing any acute symptoms. Then, after years of slowly sabotaging your happiness and overwhelming you with continuous frustration, it can even turn into the more serious condition of major depression.

Chronic discontent isn't simply a matter of negative thinking or being ungrateful. If you've suffered with it, you've probably spent a great deal of time beating yourself up for not "picking yourself up" and "being more positive." Maybe you've tried, like I did, all the self-help techniques—using positive affirmations and visualizations, gratitude journals, and meditations to change your attitude. None of it worked for long, right? That's because what you're struggling with is more than just a bad attitude about life—it is a serious condition that prevents you from experiencing much fulfillment or happiness.

You're not a loser. You're not mentally unstable. You're not a disgruntled whiner. But you *are* suffering from a condition that, if it is left untreated, can develop into a more serious psychological problem. No matter how strong an individual you might be, no one can endure the kind of continuous frustration you've known without it taking a serious toll on their life and well being.

Tom is the CEO of his own company. After years of being a traveling salesman for a software company, Tom saw a need for computer programs that would help traveling salesmen manage their business. He eventually left his employer and started his own company. Today, his company employs 300 people and is one of the largest in the field.

Even though it might look to you and me that Tom is very successful, Tom sees himself as a struggling businessman always on the verge of disaster. He works long hours, and is always on the lookout for potential crises. Most of the time his mind is totally consumed with worries about the company and its future. He pushes his staff relentlessly for more sales, higher revenue, and bigger profits.

The way Tom sees his life is that he hasn't yet "made it." When he attends conferences with other business leaders, he only sees what he hasn't yet achieved. His company hasn't earned $100 million in annual revenue. He doesn't fly on a company-owned private jet. He doesn't own homes in Aspen, the South of France, and all the other places where other CEO's own expensive real estate.

OK, so it's kind of hard to feel sorry for Tom, right? After all, if you and I had everything Tom has, we'd surely be happy. Surely.

But we wouldn't. Whether you're a CEO, a substitute teacher, a checker at the grocery store, or a stay-at-home mom, it really doesn't matter. Whatever you have or accomplish, it will always feel like less than it should when you suffer from chronic discontent. The cycle of disappointment consumes everything and colors it with frustration. Every idea that is tried, every activity . . . virtually everything disappoints you.

Clinically, chronic discontent is diagnosed as *dysthymia* or a persistent, low to moderate form of depression. While it is a form of depression, it looks and feels very different than what you might typically think of depression. In fact, many people with chronic discontent (which I will refer throughout this book as CD) suffer for years without knowing what it is that is diminishing their enjoyment of life.

Only recently has research shown that there is help for chronic discontent. Until now, CDers were the bane of the mental health profession who didn't seem to consistently respond to medication (including the popular SSRIs like Prozac) or psychotherapy. Chronic discontent was considered so difficult and frustrating to treat that many psychotherapists wouldn't agree to see a client with it. All this frustration and the lack of effective treatments lead some mental health professionals to give us derogatory labels, like "the worried well" and "neurotic cranks."

Because CD can be progressive, most people with chronic discontent don't get help until they develop a full-blown case of major depression (a distinct loss of energy, inability to concentrate, extreme weight loss or gain, hopelessness and despair, long periods of sadness and crying, etc.). Because major depression is quite treatable with a combination of medication and psychotherapy, these patients would get help and could eventually get back to normal. The problem is, normal for a person with chronic discontent isn't the normal experience of other people. It is a normal that is filled with ongoing disappointment and frustration. We are able to get through the day and function at work and home, but it is more of a struggle than it is for other people.

When someone with chronic discontent goes on to develop an instance of major depression, the technical term is "double depression." I think that term really sums up the experience—it's misery times two. The everyday experience of frustration and weariness suddenly descends into a dark cavern of hopelessness and despair. Chronic discontent that goes untreated for years often develops into a case of recurring double depression.

In fact, research strongly indicates that untreated chronic discontent is the strongest indicator of your predisposition to experience numerous major depressions in your life.

In recent years, there has been a growing interest and body of research into methods of treating chronic discontent. The research occurs under various labels with "chronic depression" and "dysthymia" the most common. More and more, there is a realization among psychotherapists that chronic discontent is a very real and widespread problem, and furthermore, that it is treatable.

As a mental health professional and former sufferer of chronic discontent, I want to share in this book what I've discovered. After finding help myself and making an exhaustive search of available research, I decided to write a book that provides useful tools in an easy to understand format. Virtually everything that is written on the subject of chronic discontent (chronic depression, dysthymia) is written for an academic/professional audience in language that is difficult to understand much less relate to your life. I wanted to write a different kind of book on the subject.

By the time you finish this book you will have all the tools you need to do the work of breaking the cycle of chronic discontent and finding some lasting contentment. It will take work and some patience, but you will find the relief you need. You can overcome chronic discontent.

What Is Chronic Discontent?

To start, let's take a closer look at just what is chronic discontent.

Do you find yourself repeatedly enthusiastic about something new in your life, only to discover that in time you completely lose the excitement and joy you once felt for it? Do you find yourself constantly looking for something else that might make you happy and fulfilled? Do you find yourself frequently bored and making changes in your life just to jump-start a better mood? Do you see yourself occasionally exploding over a small, insignificant thing that has somehow enraged you?

People with chronic discontent are often in start-up mode—first feeling good about something, but discovering that the feeling usually fades to frustration or apathy. So you start another project, relationship, job, trip, family—you name it—in search of a meaningful feeling that lasts. After repeated false starts and letdowns, you become increasingly discouraged and cynical.

Most of the time, CDers are stressed, frazzled, and frequently irritable. They feel overwhelmed and fed-up. Life has become too demanding for them, and they always seem to be just one step over their limit. They bark at their children; they snap at their mates. In short, they rarely have fun.

It's not that they want to be this way, either. Anyone who has experienced chronic discontent will tell you how guilty and ashamed they often feel for overreacting to small insignificant things. Or how much they dislike themselves for being irritable. They often long to be like other people who seem to be more carefree and fun loving.

Here are a few of the people you may recognize who suffer from chronic discontent:

- John, a 30-year-old father of three, was always starting something. One month he'd join the gym and buy all the workout paraphernalia that goes with it, only to have it stuffed in a closet a month or two later, rarely to be used again. Then he'd become obsessed with finding and buying the latest high-tech gadget that would keep his attention for a few weeks before it, too, landed in the closet. It seemed that there was always some new hobby, sport, or obsession with John, but rarely would he stick with his new interest for very long.

- Susan is the mother of two overachieving young boys. They are constantly winning awards in the classroom or on the sports field. She loves her boys, but is constantly critical of their performance. "You should have done better in algebra" she'd say, or "you were better last year at baseball than you are now." Despite the fact that her boys were extremely likeable and well behaved, she is constantly vigilant for any way they might misbehave, and is quick to correct them.

- Donna is a freelance writer who has done well for herself, although you'd never know it to hear her talk. She's placed articles in some of the best women's magazines, but she only remembers the ones that rejected her. In the supermarket line, she says to her husband, "I never figured out why they rejected that story," despite being among several magazines that had published her regularly. When she finally landed an ongoing contract with a magazine, all she could focus on was how she was paid less than someone else she knew or how great it would have been if she had a contract with this other, more popular magazine.

- Dan is a manager for a local television station. He worked hard to get where he is, especially considering he didn't graduate from college. Dan is good at what he does, but everyone around him treats him carefully. Sometimes the least little thing will set him off . . . and you don't want to be around when that happens.

- Annette just broke off her third relationship this year. Each romance felt promising from the start, but after a few months she would start to doubt her feelings and would end the relationship. She began to think that maybe there wasn't a man that she would be compatible with, or maybe she was just being too picky. She wasn't sure what the problem was, she just knew that she never seemed to fall in love with the men she dated.

John, Susan, Donna, Dan, and Annette all suffer from chronic discontent. Each in his or her own way is struggling to feel something meaningful in life, but can't. As their life progresses they are becoming increasingly frustrated and emotionally withdrawn.

So if chronic discontent is really something more than just being lazy or having a negative attitude, then what is it? What it is—and this may surprise you—is a dysfunction in the way you feel and handle your emotions. We'll look at this in more depth later in the book, but first let's look at the central role of feelings in your life.

The Bottom Line of Life

Life is about feeling. Feeling is what makes you know that you are alive. A life devoid of emotion is a life that loses the reason to continue. Feelings are just that important.

Think about this for a moment. What is it that you live for? Maybe it's the love you feel for your children. Maybe you're really passionate about your work. Maybe it's the feeling that you've done something truly worthwhile with your life.

When you see a movie or read a biography, what makes you think the story is worthwhile? When you hear an inspiring speaker, what is it about his or her message that moves you? When you decided to give money to a charity, what was it that stirred you to give? All of these things usually boil down to a feeling.

All the good things, the truly meaningful things, in life are about feeling. Dreams are wishes heavily laced with feelings. Families are started and maintained by feelings. Lasting friendships are about feelings. Even churches and synagogues are about our need to feel part of a larger whole.

Feeling is the meaning of life. If you stop feeling, your life stops having meaning to you, and you inevitably begin an earnest search to reclaim that meaning. A person who is *completely* devoid of feeling quickly becomes despondent, and can eventually become suicidal.

When you find yourself consistently frustrated as people suffering from chronic discontent do, the problem lies with your difficulty in feeling what is happening in your life. Chronic discontent isn't just feeling badly—it is difficulty feeling anything meaningful.

Caroline was a product of the go-go eighties. She entered the working world and clawed her way up the public relations ladder until she was head of a large division of a national advertising firm. Every hour of her working day was scheduled to the minute with meetings and appointments. Her hour-long commute home to the suburbs was usually spent driving with one hand while returning phone calls with the other. Although she didn't really enjoy the work, she kept telling herself things would get better with the next promotion. They never did.

When she was 38, Caroline and her husband started a family. She took off from work for six weeks after having Laura, and then returned to work at full steam. After the baby, not only did she have a demanding job, she was scheduling every minute of the day with to-do lists for the baby, shopping for meals, washing the clothes, cleaning the dishes, and all the other household duties.

After several years of this pace, Caroline realized that she wasn't happy. She had the job and family she'd always wanted, but it didn't feel like she thought it would. Her husband was the ideal for a career woman—supporting and caring—but she found herself frequently irritated with him and frequently arguing with him.

Caroline kept telling herself everything would get better when Laura started school, but it didn't. There were now car-pools, soccer games, and parent-teacher conferences. Life just kept on spinning at a mind-numbing pace, and Caroline was enjoying very little of it.

While on the surface it appears that Caroline just needed a little less stress, the truth of the matter is that she was suffering from chronic discontent and, the stress in her life, the hectic career and busy family life, was the coping mechanism for her chronic discontent. Making her life so busy was her attempt to feel something meaningful in her life. Instead, all she felt was tired and numb. Caroline was trapped in the cycle of chronic discontent.

What Exactly Are Feelings?

Feelings, in their stripped-down and most basic form, are changes that you sense in your body (for example, a change in heart rate, muscle tension, rapid breathing). Psychological research has discovered that there are only four basic feelings that meet these criteria: sad (grief), mad (anger), glad (joy), and afraid (fear or anxiety). Each of these basic feelings causes a unique, identifiable change in your body. Your heart rate may fluctuate, your muscles may become tense, and your stomach may begin to feel strange. Whatever the combination of physical changes, you have learned over the years how to clearly identify each of these four basic feelings.

What makes these physiological changes in your body happen may surprise you. The source of your feelings is a change in your body chemistry triggered most often by your *thoughts*. Of course, other things can cause your body chemistry to change and elicit feelings—like eating sugar, drinking caffeine, or taking a mood-altering drug, but in the normal course of your day it is your thoughts that most frequently cause your feelings.

Think of it this way: Imagine that you have just entered a house that you have never been in before. In another room you hear a large dog viciously growling and throwing himself against a door that leads to the room where you are. What do you feel in that moment? Most of us would feel a measure of fear, depending on how comfortable we are dealing with ferocious dogs. Some of us would be scared out of our wits.

Now imagine you learn that the dog you hear is a very realistic recording played on a stereo in the other room. What do you feel now? If you were terrified earlier, you probably feel relief now. And why? Because you had a series of thoughts that went something like this: "There's a ferocious dog in the other room that wants to do physical harm to me." Your reaction was to first feel fear, and then you thought: "It's only a tape. There is no dog. There's nothing to be afraid of here." Consequently, you no longer felt fear. Your thoughts changed, and then your feelings changed.

TFT Process

This is how the TFT process of feeling works: Thought-Feeling-Thought. You *think* "there's a vicious dog" and you *feel* afraid and then you *think* "I better get out of here." It's always thought-feeling-thought.

- You *think* "he loves me very much," and you *feel* happy, then you *think* "I want to marry him." Or, you *think* "he is getting way too clingy," and you *feel* badly, then you *think* "I've got to break up with him now."
- You *think* "my boss is deliberately trying to overwork me," and you *feel* angry, then you *think* "My boss is a jerk." Or, you *think* "my boss is in a jam and needs me to help out," and you *feel* sympathetic, then you *think* "I should stay late and help him."

Despite all the complexities of life, this basic model of feeling holds true: thought-feeling-thought. It happens with lightening speed and is usually just below the level of your awareness. This TFT process is extremely important,[1] and we'll come back to it again and again. It is the keystone that will help you understand chronic discontent and break its hold on your life.

There are a couple of very important points that you need to know about the TFT process. First, it is largely *unconscious*, meaning that it happens so automatically that you aren't aware of it happening. The thought-feeling-thought process is like a chain reaction that happens without your intervention.

---

[1] There is a great deal of clinical and scientific research to support this model. For an overview, please turn to the chapter on "Helping Those Who Help."

Once the process is triggered, the thought-feeling-thought chain clicks off without your having to do anything.

This is why "positive thinking" techniques fail to make you feel better. The TFT process is an automatic reaction, that once started cannot be consciously changed in that moment. You cannot successfully change the way you feel by forcing yourself to think happy thoughts. It just isn't that easy.

Why not? No matter what you force yourself to think about in this situation, there is something called an "automatic thought" that transpires.

Think of it this way: You really want to think that your husband isn't cheating on you, but in the back of your mind you can't forget that he has in the past. So, when he calls home to say he's coming home late, you force yourself to think "he's not cheating, he's working late" but your automatic thought is "Damn it! He's cheating on me again!" The result is that you feel anxious and sad, and then you think "I'm going to give him the third degree when he gets home!"

Automatic thoughts are the thoughts that occur to you naturally without any conscious intervention, and they are the thoughts that create the feelings in your life.

As you go through your day, make an effort to notice how you use the TFT process all the time, even in the smallest of circumstances. Becoming aware of the connection between your thoughts and your feelings is a big step in breaking the cycle of chronic discontent.

Relationships: The Crucible of Feelings

Here's another, equally critical fact about feelings. *Feelings almost always occur in the context of a relationship with another human being (this includes objects, animals, and organization to which we ascribe humanlike characteristics).* Relationships are the fiery crucible of emotion.

Think about the times in your life when you've been most overwhelmed with emotion. Picture a specific event in your life. Did it involve your relationship with another person? Most likely, it did. It was the birth, marriage, reconciliation, separation, or death of another person. Perhaps it was an event, like graduating from college after years of night school. But think carefully about this event—is it possible that what made the event so emotional for you were the people who were present? For instance, could it have been because your parents, spouse, or children were there and very proud of you?

Feelings almost always emerge out of our relationships. You can be alone and feel something, say sad or excited, but that feeling, too, usually comes from something that is happening in one of your relationships—or maybe even the lack of a relationship. Perhaps it is a sad feeling about a troubling disagreement with your spouse or a joyous feeling about a successful business deal with a client. Feelings occur either directly because of a relationship or an event that has affected a relationship.

This is an extremely important point and worth pausing to consider. *Feelings are almost always triggered by a relationship.* It is a fact that goes against the grain of our "rugged individual" view that posits us as being strong, independent, and capable of functioning completely alone if necessary. In order to feel, we need other people. Furthermore, since we've seen that feeling is central to the meaning of life, we can say that *we need other people to find meaning in our lives.*

Consider, if you will, that biologists have long accepted human beings as "social animals" who function best in a group of other human beings. We are born into a family, and when most of us reach adulthood, we marry another person and establish our own family. We keep in touch with a circle of friends, many of whom we've known for most of our lives. We choose to live in cities and communities with other people. We work in organizations or in close contact with other people. We are, by all definitions, social creatures.

Our individual biology is wired to need and respond to other human beings. One of the primary ways our bodies respond to other humans is through feelings. In fact, evolutionists consider emotions as adaptive self-preservation. Our feelings help us to function successfully with other human beings. We need other people, and they need us. Feelings make this possible.

When we experience problems with our feelings, it is almost related to a problem with our relationships. Either we are struggling to form strong relationships or a previously effective relationship is no longer available.

Briefly, let me mention the idea of "codependence" and how this fits into the picture. Because of the widespread understanding of the negative effect of codependence, many people and even some mental health professionals are slow to acknowledge the basic need each of us has for other human beings. In reality, these two things are not contradictory at all. Codependence refers to the negative effectives of extreme dependence upon another person. Think of it this way—codependence is to relationships what obesity is to a healthy diet. It is the result of getting "too much of a good thing"—in this case, too much of the dependence and emotion that make relationships so central and satisfying in our lives.

Before we move on to the final concept in this chapter, let's go back and connect what we've covered so far. First, we saw that feelings come from automatic thoughts. Second, we saw that feelings also come from relationships. Are these two points contradictory?

Not at all. We can synthesize the truth of these statements by saying that feelings come from thoughts about others and ourselves in a relationship. Let me illustrate this:

- You think: "My business is failing, and therefore I can't support my family." Then you feel terrible.
- You think: "A wonderful man has asked me to marry him." Then you feel joyous.
- You think: "I'm failing this class, and my parents/spouse/fellow students will think that I'm a loser." Then you feel sad.

Even when you're not immediately aware of it, the thoughts that produce your feelings are about a relationship between yourself and another person.

Maybe you're wondering, isn't it possible to feel disappointed in myself for a failure or to feel proud of myself for an accomplishment? Of course you can. But if you take a second look at those feelings, you'll see that an automatic component of the thought that produced the feeling has to do with the effect on your relationships. Perhaps the achievement will make you more desirable and lovable, or perhaps the failure will make you less so.

If at this point you find yourself still a bit cautious about acknowledging that all your feelings emerge from relationships, all I ask is that you accepted it loosely for the time being. As you and I progress down this journey, I think you'll find it more acceptable down the road from here.

Remembered Feelings

Past relationships leave you with *remembered feelings*. Your brain contains a special memory for past emotions. The time you were scolded for eating ice cream before dinner. The time your boyfriend dumped you for another woman. The time you gave birth to your first child. These and many more remembered feelings are stored away in your emotional memory. Remembered feelings are the memory of feelings that you once felt.

Remembered feelings have something that psychologists describe as "tags." Simply put, whenever something happens to you that was similar to what has happened to you before, it activates the tag, causing you to feel the remembered feeling. Suddenly, in the present moment you are feeling a lesser version of what you once experienced in a similar situation. For example, when your fiancé takes you to a nice restaurant and says, "I want to tell you something," you panic, remembering the feeling of being dumped by a boyfriend years earlier in a similar setting.

Remembered feelings become stronger the more we engage them. In other words, if your mother used to punish you when your room wasn't clean, you feel uncomfortable in untidy places. Every time you recall that emotional memory by feeling uncomfortable in an untidy place, you strengthen that memory, making it more likely to occur again. It's just like any other memory—the more you recall it, the longer the memory remains with you. Likewise, when you haven't recalled a particular memory for many years, it begins to fade and becomes increasingly more difficult to recall.

One of the most powerful remembered feelings is *shame*. Shame is the memory of feeling sad and angry about something in your past. When you forgot how to spell a simple word in the regional spelling bee, you felt embarrassed, sad, and maybe even angry at yourself. Today, whenever you fail at a simple task, you are flooded with shame—a feeling that has its roots in your distant past.

Shame plays a powerful role in the development and ongoing influence of chronic discontent in your life. It is a powerful remembered feeling that may have shaped much of your current life. In the upcoming chapters, we'll look more closely at the shame in your life.

Remembered feelings are often at the center of life problems. You may fall in love with someone because they triggered romance feelings from a past relationship or you may explode in anger over a situation that doesn't deserve such a response, but has triggered some past painful, emotional memory.

The problem with remembered feelings is that they cloud and confuse the primary feelings of the moment. In other words, you may not really enjoy the company of someone you're dating, but because this person triggers remembered feelings that are positive, you conclude that you feel good about the romance. Remembered feelings can significantly color the way you perceive your feelings, and without them, you might feel differently, act differently, and ultimately create a different life for yourself.

2

A High Emotional Threshold

What are you feeling right at this very moment?

Can you describe the feeling without having to "think up" an answer?

If you're like most people with chronic discontent, you have difficulty knowing what you feel in any ordinary moment. Given a few seconds, you could probably describe a feeling, but only after you thought it over.

How do I know this? There are many ways I've come to know this, not the least of which was my own struggle with chronic discontent. For years I worked my way through a profession where one is *supposed* to be "in touch" with one's feelings. I wasn't. I could compose lots of wonderfully sounding phrases that described feelings—but they were not my feelings. I had read extensively about the varieties of emotions and how people experience these emotions, but it was only another psychological fact that I stored in my brain. In reality, I had little personal experience with the subject I was so diligently studying.

A High Emotional Threshold

I often wondered what was wrong with me—why I didn't seem to feel things as intensely as other people. Why was I bored, feeling nothing of significance, so much of the time?

Since the beginning of my career, I had worked with many clients who suffered from oversensitivity to their emotions, individuals who were quickly overwhelmed by their feelings and unable to function in a healthy way (this is a component of many well-researched psychological disorders). I knew that these clients suffered from an inability to filter out unwanted or trivial emotions. But what about those of us who seemed to be *less* sensitive than most other people to emotions? Isn't it possible that we also suffered, but in a very different way? It seemed to me that just as many people suffered from the inability to feel, but far less was written about these clients.

It was clear to me (as it is for many researchers now, too) that this was about *emotional thresholds*, or the point at which emotions become felt. Some had low emotional thresholds (highly sensitive to our emotions) and others, like me, had high emotional thresholds (less sensitive to our emotions).

Your body has many different kinds of thresholds. For example, you have an auditory threshold which is the decibel level at which a sound becomes loud enough that you can hear it, and a tactile threshold which is the temperature at which a substance begins to feel hot or cold to you. An *emotional threshold* is the intensity that your feelings must reach in order to enter into your awareness. In other words, the point at which you begin to feel a feeling.

Think of it this way. You are driving home from work in traffic that becomes increasingly heavier. At first, you don't notice that you're feeling anxious about the traffic, but as you continue home and the traffic gets worse, you become aware of your anxiety about the traffic. The point at which your anxiety became intense enough to enter your awareness is your emotional threshold.

Some people become aware of this kind of anxiety almost immediately. Others aren't aware of it until it becomes very intense. All other things being equal, the first kind of person has a low emotional threshold and the second has a high emotional threshold.

A low emotional threshold means that even the most slight or insignificant emotions are felt, often with a greater intensity than the emotion warrants. The experience of a low emotional threshold is to be swamped with feelings, even to the point of occasionally being incapacitated from experiencing so many emotions. As you can imagine, having a low emotional threshold can create a great deal of psychological suffering.

But what about those of us who are on the other side of that continuum with a high emotional threshold? It only makes sense that we, too, might experience some difficulty in life. Rather than being overwhelmed with too many emotions, we walk through life struggling to feel something worthwhile.

This is the condition of chronic discontent: a high emotional threshold. My experience of emotions was limited to only occasional, intense feelings. Most of the time, I really didn't feel much of anything. I bored easily, and if I felt anything it was most often frustration.

I longed to feel something intensely. I longed for lasting satisfaction and fulfillment. I wished I could continue to feel love as I did when I first fell in love—a feeling that had become nothing more than a memory. I often felt as if I were viewing a Technicolor world through a black-and-white viewer. Everyone else seemed to have a much richer experience of life than did I.

But how does this condition start? Can a person lower their

emotional threshold? These questions are of great importance to all of us who suffer from chronic discontent. To begin with, let's take a close look at how you developed a high emotional threshold.

Thou Shalt Not Feel

For most CDers, the problem was that we learned feelings were shameful at a young age. Emotions were messy, noisy, distracting, distasteful things that were not to be expressed in polite company. Instead of experiencing our true feelings, we learned to hide them from the world around us.

For example, John suffers from chronic discontent, and as a child had a fairly strict upbringing. If he did make the mistake of expressing a feeling that was less than desirable, presentable, or that was inconsistent with his mother's feelings, he was punished. For example, if he was unhappy at an inconvenient time for his parents, he was told that he was bad. If he was feeling joyful and too rowdy, he was told to go to his room and settle down. When he wanted to slack off from schoolwork and just hang out with his friends, he was told that he was lazy and should be doing something more productive. When he just wanted to watch "I Love Lucy" and laugh at Lucy's silly antics, he was sternly reminded that he should be doing better things with his time than watching "the tube."

The cumulative effect of all these messages was to teach him two things: 1) He should never trust his feelings for they would always lead him astray, and 2) He should only allow himself to feel "good" feelings.

In short, he was taught that there are good feelings and bad feelings. Good people only had good feelings. Desperate as any child is to please his caregivers, he bought the story completely. He convinced himself (as do most people with chronic discontent) that his problem was that he was feeling the wrong feelings, and tried to only feel the "good" feelings.

So he did what all chronically discontent persons learn to do at some point to do—he learned to avoid feeling as much as possible. It wasn't easy, but over the years he learned how to do it. Whenever he began to feel that rise of his feelings, he employed a number of techniques to distract himself from it until it subsided. He shut down that part of himself that thrived on feelings and learned to function without it. The only feelings that made it through the virtually impenetrable wall he created were strong feelings of anger, and on rare occasions, love or joy. During those few times when he was overcome by those strong bursts of feeling, he felt overwhelmed and extremely guilty. It made him very uncomfortable to be under the influence of his emotions and as quickly as he could, he would try to regain control and be more "rational."

John's experience isn't unique. Virtually every adult who suffers from chronic discontent reports the same experience—learning to shut down the feeling side of themselves because they felt uncomfortable and guilty during the rare moments when they were flooded with emotion.

Your Emotional Muscle

Think of the ability to feel as a muscle—the more you exercise it, the better you become at it. For example, if you want to be a graceful ice skater, then you must exercise the muscles that are used in skating. The more you exercise, the more you are able to make difficult movements, and consequently, the better you skate.

So it is with feeling. The more you exercise your ability to feel, the better you become. You understand your feelings, recognize the subtle differences (for example, between frustration and legitimate anger), and know which feelings are best to "sit with" and those which should be acted upon. Conversely, the longer you deny, avoid, and belittle your feelings, the more your ability to handle your feelings falters. With enough emotional neglect, you can severely impair your ability to feel.

Remember the TFT process of feelings? This process is the "muscle" part of feeling. Some people who have well developed emotional "muscle" have a great deal of practice with TFT process. Their TFT process allows them to discriminate between fine differences of feelings and emotions. For example, they don't just feel sad, they actually feel the difference between gloomy, distressed, and upset. These are different experiences for them because they have a highly developed TFT process that provides them a rich experience of their feelings.

But this is not the case for those of us suffering with chronic discontent. We know that we feel sad, but not much more than that. Sometimes we can't even put our finger on how it is that we feel—we just know that we don't feel too great. Right?

Because people with chronic discontent avoid situations that trigger feelings, we rarely exercise our TFT process, and consequently, it isn't very well developed. We mentally withdraw from emotionally charged situations—leave the room as it were—to avoid making ourselves feel. The ways in which we withdraw are quite varied, and don't necessarily require physically leaving a situation. Most often, it involves emotionally withdrawing by automatically changing our thoughts to something different, far removed from the situation we are in.

Throughout this book, we'll return to the emotional muscle analogy often. It's a helpful way to think about your ability to feel. Toward the end of this book, we'll look at a number of exercises that will help you strengthen your ability to feel and consequently lower your emotional threshold.

There is one feeling, however, that persists even when you haven't exercised your ability to feel. That feeling is *frustration*—a complex emotion that has at its core the primary emotion of anger. The fact is, CDers are almost always lost in a sea of frustration over what their life has become.

Why? Frustration is a natural reaction at not having your emotional appetite satisfied. Frustration grows as your emotional needs go unmet until it becomes so great that it exceeds your high emotional threshold. Suddenly, you find yourself overwhelmed with frustration.

People with chronic discontent expect to be frustrated by new things, even before they try them. The new job probably isn't going to work out and the new boss will likely be a jerk. The new boyfriend will probably turn out to be a loser like all the rest. The car mechanic will probably be dishonest. The class will probably be boring and the teacher uninspiring.

You know the story well—everything is laced with frustration. During the years I suffered from chronic discontent I expected the worst from almost everything I did. Years of experience had taught me that whatever I did eventually lost its luster and became devoid of meaning for me. Sooner or later, I would find myself frustrated and angry.

So I changed jobs, moved to another city, and started a new relationship all in an effort to fill the growing void within me. Nothing seemed to work. I started wondering what was so wrong with me that I couldn't find some lasting happiness and fulfillment. My self-confidence began to slip as my frustration increased.

My closest friends began to notice that every conversation eventually turned negative with me. I was always the first to point out why something wouldn't work or to find the negative aspect of their successes. I knew something was wrong, but what?

Most people who come to therapy with chronic discontent are at this point. They are overwhelmed with frustration, but don't know what is causing it. They feel empty inside and long for some lasting happiness. The frustration drives them to seek help.

Because CDers become negative and critical of others, other people begin to move away from you. You look for the worst in others, and usually find it. As a result, you must change your group of friends every few years.

This is one of the debilitating paradoxes of chronic discontent: Feelings occur most often in relationships, yet as your chronic discontent progresses, you move farther away from other people. The more frustrated and cynical you become, the more others avoid you, and the worse off you are. Inadvertently, you destroy your relationships, leaving you with less opportunity to feel much of anything but rejected and lonely.

3

A Deep Hunger

You really wanted the new car, but now you're thinking of selling it.

You really wanted to have a relationship with your new squeeze, but now you're not so sure about it.

You really wanted to change careers, but the new one isn't working out so great.

What is it that you really, really want? Do you know?

At this point, you probably don't know. You've tried everything you can think of and none of it worked, right?

What you really want are relationships that are emotionally open and honest. You are starved for relationships that fulfill your need for emotional "flow," and you've tried everything else in your bag of tricks to try to fill this need with no success. The new car, the job, the relationship, the move—all of them were attempts to fill this basic craving inside you, and none of them worked.

Emotionally Honest Relationships

Emotionally honest relationships have two important components: connection and flow. Connection occurs in the beginning of a relationship and is the process of discovering
common values and interests. Chances are, you are good at
making connections with other people.

- You have your bowling buddies.
- You enjoy coffee with the ladies from church.
- You get along well with your friends in the book club.
- You golf regularly with your business associates.

After we meet someone, we either make a connection or
we don't. Sometimes we meet a business customer and are
friendly with one another, but don't discover any common
ground between us. These kinds of "unconnected" relationships can function quite well for basic and routine transactions.

- You wave to her once a week when you pick up her
  kids for carpool, but never really say much to one
  another.
- You call him every time the copier breaks down, and
  he takes care of it immediately but you don't know
  much about him.
- They are both friendly neighbors, but you never share
  more than small talk on the front yard.

Those of us with chronic discontent fill our lives with connected and unconnected relationships. In our connected relationships, we share a common hobby, religious beliefs, or career
interests, for example. We talk about these things, and perhaps

even feel a bond of closeness because we share a common interest. In our unconnected relationships, we are friendly and communicative, but never move beyond being acquaintances. Into these two categories fall most of our relationships.

Emotionally honest relationships, however, go beyond connection and include "flow." Flow is the process of honest and authentic emotional exchange between two people who have already established a connection. Flow means that we can share our intimate dreams, fears, thoughts and pasts. Flow means we allow ourselves to be fully present for another person, without hiding or editing who we are. When experiencing flow with another person, we are free to express exactly what we feel, regardless of what it is.

Flow is what those of us with chronic discontent don't have. We make a connection, sometimes a very solid connection, but always stop short of flow. We hold back, edit, and sometimes even disguise our real feelings. Flow feels dangerous to us, and we stop short of it every time.

The experience of flow in a relationship is deeply satisfying. There's no doubt that you have experienced it at some point in your life. When you think back on an experience where you freely shared your feelings with someone who did the same with you, it was a meaningful and treasured encounter. Flow feeds a deep craving within us all.

The process of connection and flow is essential to emotionally honest relationships. When we allow both to happen, it immediately dissipates the feelings of discontent and frustration that haunt you. Suddenly, you feel alive and rejuvenated. Flow is both the source and the stage for meaningful, lasting feelings.

For the first time in his life, Roger felt really wonderful about his relationship with his father. It was a strange way for

Roger to feel, since his father was recovering from heart surgery, but for the first time they really talked to each other.

Roger's father had always been the strong, silent type of man. He didn't talk much, and when he did, it wasn't about his feelings. Roger remembers that as a child he respected and even feared his father, but it was with his mother he went to when he needed help or was in trouble. He knew his father loved him, but couldn't ever remember him saying so.

After the surgery, Roger's father had insisted that Roger be the one to sit with him through the night. All night he talked, and told Roger how proud he was of him, about how sorry he was that he hadn't been there for Roger more, and how happy he was that Roger was with him now. They talked about Roger's life, his dreams, and even the business failure when he lost most of his savings a few years back. For the first time, Roger told his father how much he loved him.

After Roger's father recovered from the surgery, their relationship returned to what it had been, but Roger remembers that night fondly. For the first, and perhaps only time, he experienced flow with his father.

Once Upon a Time

Those of us with chronic discontent remember discrete experiences of flow in our closest relationships. Flow isn't an ongoing experience for us; it is something that happens very rarely and only under special circumstances.

Because we are starved for flow, when it does happen to us, it changes our lives. We decide to marry the person. Or, we become friends for life. However we react to it, it invariably becomes one of our treasured memories. For example:

- Janet remembers the night during a high school ski trip when she and Theresa stayed up most of the night talking. She'd always been friendly with Theresa, but never really connected with her. That night they talked about everything—boyfriends, parents, college. . . . Then, a few weeks later, they both went off to different colleges, both eventually married, and they now live more than a thousand miles away from each other. Janet still keeps up with Theresa and considers her one of her closest friends.

- The day that Ron and Sue spent hiking through the mountains was the day Ron decided to ask Sue to marry him. He had never felt so close to anyone in his life. On that day, he felt like he could talk about anything with Sue.

Experiences of flow are milestones for people with chronic discontent, and not a regular experience. It feels so wonderful and fulfilling that it affects us in a memorable way.

Feeling content, however, requires that we have the ongoing experience of flow in our lives. Not just with one person, but to be surrounded by people with whom we share this uninterrupted flow. The flow both allows us to feel deeply and feeds us. Without it, we sink slowly into the mire of discontent.

The Lifeline

A common technique that many CDers have used to simulate flow, is to create what I call the emotional "lifeline." The emotional lifeline is one person in life with whom we have a strong connection, and perhaps even, on rare occassions, experience flow. The connection with this special person, while not completely fulfilling, helps to maintain our emotional equilibrium.

For many people with chronic discontent, the emotional lifeline is with their life partner. The relationship is close in the sense that they talk about the events of life but stop short of real emotional honesty. The emotional lifeline helps to fill the void created in our lives by not having flow. The relationship shares a pseudo-emotional honesty that doesn't really fulfill us, but keeps us from being swallowed by feelings of loneliness and despair. If the emotional lifeline is broken, we find ourselves desperate to replace it.

Linda and Jimmy had been married for more than twenty years when he suddenly died of a heart attack. Their marriage, while comfortable, hadn't been intimate for many years. Although they never discussed it, they had become more like two old friends who loved their children and lived together.

After Jimmy's death, Linda became increasingly consumed with loneliness and grief. She felt as if she couldn't function without Jimmy and eventually began thinking of suicide. Life without him was just too difficult.

A year after Jimmy's death, Wess, an old high school boyfriend, called Linda. His wife had died a few years earlier and Linda and Wess began seeing one another. Within three months, they married.

When the emotional lifeline is broken, as it was for Linda, CDers are thrust into a desperate situation. While the lifeline never really gave them the emotional honesty they craved, it did fill that place in their lives and helped to combat the feelings of loneliness and isolation. While the lifeline relationship isn't emotionally fulfilling, it is necessary to keep the CDer functioning in life.

A Living Network

The research is indisputably clear on this point: you need a network of relationships that are open, honest, and supportive to be healthy and happy. Rarely is anything so clearly evident from divergent research. You need to experience more than just connections, you need to regularly experience flow from more than just one person in your life. You need a living network of relationships that allow you to express and validate your feelings freely and completely.

Chronic discontent is a disease that cripples our ability to create this living network. We make connections with other people; in fact, we may even be quite outgoing and social, but we stop short of creating the intimacy necessary for emotional flow.

Emotional Dishonesty

The block we create to emotional flow is best described as *emotional dishonesty*. Emotional dishonesty ranges from simply hiding our true feelings from others to actively falsifying our feelings in ways that may be more acceptable and less confrontational.

If you're like most of us, using the word "dishonest" to describe yourself is difficult, if not downright offensive. None of us wants to think of ourselves as dishonest.

But CDers are, all the time. We hide our true feelings from other people when those feelings aren't convenient or might be uncomfortable. When it's to our advantage, we sometimes even fake more acceptable feelings for the benefit of others.

You must own your emotional dishonesty if you want to break the hold of chronic discontent on your life. These are strong words, but important. There's simply no other way.

We can all laugh about our intentional emotional dishonesty when a good friend asks "does this make me look fat?" or when we've been invited to a dinner party where the host has put a great deal of effort into a meal that turns out badly. We smile and say harmlessly, "What a delicious meal!"

The kind of emotional dishonesty that really gets us into trouble goes much deeper. It is the buried resentments at the spouse who continually takes us for granted. It is the unexpressed anger at an over-controlling parent. It is the hidden loss of affection and attraction for your lover. These and a whole host of other deep feelings are suppressed and hidden because the consequences of those feelings terrify us.

Whether the emotional lie is small or large, an omission or deception, it blocks the emotional flow. It prevents us from creating the kinds of relationships that are truly fulfilling.

Just in case you were raised, as I was, to be always polite—even if you had to lie about something to "spare" another's feelings—you need to understand that emotionally honesty isn't necessarily harmful or deliberately cruel. Even when the situation requires you to express a difficult or painful feeling, there is always a compassionate way to do it. You can always tell someone how you feel without being mean or overly hurtful about it.

Joan admitted that she had gained an extra forty pounds and virtually lost all interest in having sex, but the day that her husband, Nick, sat down and told her just that, and furthermore, that he wasn't attracted to her as he used to be was one of the most painful days she can remember.

"I cried for days. I packed my suitcase to leave Nick three different times. I gave him the cold shoulder and stopped doing anything around the house. Then, something inside me clicked. God, I didn't want to admit it, but he was right. I had really let myself go. Who would be attracted to this? For heaven's sake, I couldn't bear to see myself nude in the mirror!"

After grieving over the trouble in her marriage, Joan joined a weight clinic and a gym. She didn't go overboard with it, but after nine months she had lost the weight and was looking like a new woman. Nick was amazed at the transformation and couldn't get enough of her.

What do you suppose would have happened if Nick hadn't expressed his feelings to Joan? Inevitably, they would have grown apart, one or both of them might have sought out an affair. Perhaps they would have stayed together amicably or perhaps divorced. Who knows?

Maybe you're thinking, "Nick should have loved her just the way she was!" That's a nice sentiment, but it isn't the way human beings work. We don't feel the "should's." We all should like many things that we don't. Likewise, we all like many things that we shouldn't. Feelings don't obey our self-imposed should's and should-not's.

A typical CDer would probably feel shame for feeling that she wasn't attracted to her spouse, tell herself "I should love my husband just like he is!" and would try to suppress the feeling. Of course, the feeling doesn't go away, the emotional dishonesty only creates a further block between her and her spouse. The temporary benefit of swallowing a difficult feeling only creates more serious problems down the road.

Emotional dishonesty can take many forms, and we'll explore these throughout this book. Confronting emotional dishonesty however it appears and eliminating it from our behavior is crucial to overcoming chronic discontent.

4

The Early Seeds of Discontent

The seeds of chronic discontent are often planted deeply in your unconscious mind very early in life. Carlo Lorenzini unintentionally chronicles this process in his classic tale *The Adventures of Pinocchio*. In that popular children's tale, the wood carver Geppetto decides to create a wooden puppet for himself. The puppet he names Pinocchio.

Pinocchio, we are told, is an impudent puppet who refuses to be controlled by others, and instead follows his feelings. His feelings immediately get him into serious trouble, and Pinocchio's journey becomes a child's nightmare:

- He is overjoyed by music he hears coming from a marionette theater, but is quickly overtaken by the director of the show who attempts to use Pinocchio as firewood.
- He trusts the Fox and the Cat, who immediately betray his trust by robbing him and eventually trying to kill him.
- He gives in to the thrill of an amusement park and is straightway turned into a donkey.

- As a donkey, he refused to perform humiliating circus tricks, which results in his being thrown off a cliff and swallowed by a shark.
- All throughout his journey, a cricket keeps shaming him for following his feelings, telling him that he is "a rascal of the worst kind . . . rude, lazy, a runaway."

It isn't until Pinocchio's free spirit is broken, and he is willing to return home to live as Geppetto dictates that he is made into a real boy. Ironically, it is only once he becomes an emotional puppet that he is considered a "real boy" in the story.

Have you never thought of the story of Pinocchio in this way? Does it trouble you to see such dark messages hidden in a beloved children's story? If you're like most of us, you thought it was just a tale about the evil consequences of lying.

Interestingly enough, Pinocchio learned to lie so he could function in a world where he wasn't free to express and follow his feelings. Early in his journey he discovered that emotional honesty was often punished, and so he tried to survive by hiding the truth. If you read the story again as an adult, you can feel yourself sympathizing with the poor puppet's pathetic lies.

There's another part of this story that is extremely important, and often missed by those who "clean-up" the original text for today's audiences. Geppetto was clearly a very angry man who was known to punish children severely. In the English translation, bystanders say of Geppetto and Pinocchio:

"Poor Marionette," called out a man. "I am not surprised he doesn't want to go home. Geppetto, no doubt, will beat him unmercifully, he is so mean and cruel!"

"Geppetto looks like a good man," added another, "but with boys he's a real tyrant. If we leave that poor Marionette in his hands he may tear him to pieces."[2]

Here we begin to see the dark truth of the story. The process of hardening your senses to your own emotions often starts in childhood, like it did in this story for Pinocchio. Parents, teachers, and others influential adults may have taught you—perhaps even physically punished you—for expressing your feelings. Feelings, you may have been told, are evil and will lead you into a life of a "scoundrel."

The Messages of Emotional Shame

As in this simple childhood story, the messages of emotional hardening and chronic discontent were planted in your young life in subtle ways. The result in adulthood is that you survive by shutting down your ability to feel, leaving you much like a wooden shell of a person who is desperately trying to regain the joy of living. You become that emotional puppet, only mimicking the "good" feelings.

Whatever your childhood experience was, as an adult you've learned to shame yourself mercilessly for your feelings. The few times you've burst into tears in front of someone else, weren't you mortally ashamed and found you had to avoid them in the future? Aren't you extremely resistant to the important people in your life seeing you express joy or exhilaration? Don't you avoid situations where there will be strong, unbridled emotions directed at you, like heated arguments, or heart-to-heart talks?

[2]*The Adventures of Pinocchio*, C. Collodi (pseudonym for Carlo Lorenzini).

These experiences are *emotional shame*. They are times when you are ashamed and maybe even fearful of your emotions. When you feel humiliated, ashamed, or guilty for expressing a genuine emotion you are engaging the shame you have learned about your feelings.

Think about this for a moment. No matter what emotion you are expressing, why should you be ashamed of something that emerges from the deepest part of yourself? Why do you worry about what others will think of you if they see such an intimate part of yourself? Will they belittle you for feeling that way? Will they embarrass or humiliate you? Will they somehow use that information to hurt you?

If your first reaction is to say "yes" to any of these questions, then you've got to ask yourself one more. Do you continue to surround yourself with people who continue to shame you for your feelings? If so, then you've experienced firsthand how shame can live one, long past the place where it started.

When you really step back and look at it, it is easy to see how destructive shame is, isn't it? But seeing this alone doesn't change anything. Shame is a remembered feeling that doesn't change just because you know it isn't OK. The fact is, shame takes a great deal of time and effort to be resolved. It won't go away overnight, no matter how many insights you have. You've got to confront it over and over again before it finally loses its stranglehold on your life.

For now, let's look at how emotional shame manifests in your life. Remember those times when you were mortified by expressing something you felt? Can you remember afterward how embarrassed and ashamed you felt at having those feelings?

For men, those feelings of shame often occur around crying or being vulnerable in front of other people. For women, the shame often occurs around times of expressing anger or unrequited affection. Whatever the situation, I'll bet you can recall those feelings of shame quite vividly. Let me share with you a story of one person and the emotional shame he lives with:

"When I was a teenager, I spent most of my free time at the local scout hut. It wasn't far from my home . . . I could ride my bike there in a matter of minutes. The scout troop was always doing something fun. We had weekly meetings every Tuesday night to plan our next camping, fishing, or hiking trip. All of us in the troop were like brothers . . . we had been together for more than four years, and even though we didn't always get along, we were very close.

"I was especially close to John who was assistant patrol leader with me. Over the junior high years we became best friends, spending most of our time at school and afterward together. John was the first really close friend I had and since I didn't have a brother in my family, I considered John my brother.

"One day after school we were riding our bikes near the river . . . I can remember it very well . . . when John told me that his Dad had been transferred to a town that was about an hour away. It was only a few weeks before they would move away.

"The day that they packed the moving van, I was over at John's house. When they finally pulled down the street, I was so upset that I rode home crying. When I got home, my Dad happened to be there. He was furious with me for crying and told me that young men didn't cry in public and that he was ashamed of me. Some things, he said, you just have to take like a man. And more than anything, I wanted to be like a man, like him.

"I was so embarrassed; I can hardly talk about it. To this day, I feel my face flush when I think about it. I was totally humiliated. Now, I can't cry . . . in private or public."

Here's an important starting point: Feelings are never wrong. Never. Feelings are valid and worthwhile simply because you feel them. Not all feelings come from the moment in which they are experienced—some are connected to events that have long ago passed, but the emotional memory is still very active. Like in the example above, the memory of being shamed for crying as a boy is still active in this man's adult life. Whenever he feels upset, especially in public, he feels weak and shameful. Why? It's the legacy of a remembered feeling.

The Essence of Shame

Let's take a closer look at the mechanics of how your feelings so quickly turn into shame. It's all about a corrupting influence in your TFT process. All strong feelings trigger thoughts of shame. No matter what the feeling is, whether it be joy or sorrow, you find yourself chastising yourself for feeling it.

It happens through a process that psychologists call *conditioning*. Conditioning is nothing more than the pairing of two events over time. The way it works is, as time goes on, the first event starts to elicit the second event.

This really is pretty simple. You may remember the classical example of Pavlov's dogs where a tone was paired with food so often that eventually the dogs expected food every time they heard a tone. Or how John B. Watson conditioned a young boy to fear bunny rabbits by always sounding a loud noise whenever the boy attempted to play with the rabbit. (It was a cruel experiment, but somehow made it into just about every psychology 101 textbook.)

This is exactly how you were conditioned to be ashamed of your feelings. When you expressed joy, you were scolded for acting foolish. Or, whenever you fell in love, your heart was soon afterward broken. Your feelings became paired with a self-debasing thought. That thought, in turn, elicited feelings of shame.

In time, the pairing of your feelings and those self-debasing thoughts became a conditioned response—something of a psychological reflex. They happen so closely together in time that you experience them as one event.

- You think, "I finally graduated!" and you feel exhilarated, and then scold yourself for acting childishly (e.g., dancing wildly at the graduation party).
- You think, "This is the best guy I've met in a long time," and you feel love, and then think "I'll probably be rejected."
- You think, "I'll never be able to hear Mom's voice again, now that she's gone," and you feel deep grief that causes you to sob uncontrollably, and then think "I am weak and powerless because I feel this way."

Consequently, strong feelings become associated with remembered feelings of foolishness, rejection, weakness, powerlessness—in short, shame.

Think about your reaction to feeling. What's going through your mind when you start to cry at a sad movie? ("I can't cry here—people will think I'm silly and weak.") Or when you feel really excited and happy over an unexpected accomplishment at work? ("I must keep my professional demeanor or people will think I've lost control.")

Over time, the shame begins to have a deep and tragic effect on your life. For example, difficult conversations with your spouse that make one or both of you cry make you feel incredibly shameful. Or, maybe when you tell your partner that you love him or her it floods you with the feeling of shame and embarrassment. (This is a sad and very common reaction of my patients with CD.)

So the feeling process of thought-feeling-thought becomes one of thought—feeling—shame (e.g., I'm foolish, weak, bad, etc. for feeling this way). The feeling immediately triggers the remembered feeling of shame. As soon as you feel something meaningful, you chastise yourself mentally.

You don't have to be shamed by something too many times in your life, before you learn to think ahead and avoid whatever has caused you shame in the past. So the corrupted TFT process actually causes you to avoid situations that might evoke feeling. Hence, you come to the place in life where you experience less emotion, effectively raising your emotional threshold.

- You feel exhilarated, and then scold yourself for acting childishly—*in the future, you avoid situations where you may feel exhilarated.*
- You feel love, and then think "I'll probably be rejected."—*in the future, you avoid loving relationships.*
- You feel grief, and then think "I am weak and powerless because I feel this way."—*in the future, you refuse to allow yourself to grieve.*

The result is that first you *escape* feeling situations (just like a child will jump back after touching a hot stove), and from that point forward, you *avoid* those situations altogether (the child never touches a hot stove again). You start to recognize a feeling welling up inside you, and immediately try to escape the situation so the feeling doesn't engulf you. It doesn't take too many experiences of that remembered feeling of shame to clobber you, before you learn to avoid your feelings, and thus avoid the shame that would follow the feeling.

It's just a basic rule of nature: you naturally avoid those things that have punished you before. *Your feelings trigger remembered feelings of shame, so you try to avoid your feelings and thus the punishing feeling of shame that follows.*

The Nature of Avoidance

Avoiding your feelings can have a deeply troubling effect on your life. For example:

- You don't think about your troubled marriage because it makes you feel helpless and sad. To help you not think about the marriage, you avoid intimate conversations with your spouse, refuse to go to marriage counseling, or perhaps even limit the amount of time alone with your spouse.
- You don't think about your dead-end job because it makes you feel like a loser. To help you not think about the job, you spend as little time as you can at work, and only do the minimum that is required of you. Any chance you have to "goof off," you take full advantage of it.
- You don't think about the abuse you lived through as a child because it makes you feel afraid and very sad. To help you do this, you avoid relationships that become too intimate or relationships with powerful people who remind you of the abuser.

Sometimes, you are in a situation where it is difficult not to think about things that elicit strong feelings. Take for example when your wife confronts you about your lack of emotional participation in the marriage. What do you do now? Quite simply, you mentally change the channel, if you can't physically leave the situation. You try to change the subject or tune out your wife's complaints. For example, you might think about how much your wife whines (instead of your own lack of active involvement in the relationship), and rather than answering her concerns, you attack her for being a "whiner" who is never happy with anything. By changing the channel, you can effectively withdraw from the situation and avoid painful feelings.

To summarize this process, here's a diagram that illustrates the way it works:

We think, then we feel, then we think something like "Whoa! This is about to get heavy. I'd better get out of here." And then we *withdraw*. We leave the room, change our thoughts, or do something to disturb the situation—anything to escape those feelings.

Here's how the chronic discontent TFT process might be experienced:

Instead of staying with the feeling and handling it productively:

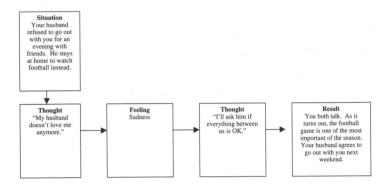

It is the remembered feeling of shame that you have long associated with feelings that causes you to withdraw rather than handle the feeling productively as in this example. The feeling of sadness over a relationship that has difficulties is "unbearable" to you because the feeling is attached to such discomfort and shame in your past.

Russell was a veteran of the Vietnam War, and ever since his tour of duty in the armed services, he suffered from chronic discontent (coupled with post-traumatic stress disorder). When Russell was in his mid-forties, his father, with whom he was very close, died suddenly of a massive heart attack. Russell, completely unable to deal with the powerful feelings of grief that the memories of his father evoked, tried to lose himself completely in taking care of the details of funeral. By filling his mind with these practical matters, he could avoid the thoughts that would bring him tremendous sorrow.

After the funeral, when all the family gathered back at his mother's home and there was nothing left for Russell to attend to, thoughts and memories of his father began to flood his mind. The terror of those feelings was so great, that he literally fainted as he stepped out of the car in front of his mother's house. When all else had failed him, Russell physically withdrew by fainting. It wasn't necessarily a conscious choice of Russell's, but none the less was an avoidance strategy that his unconscious mind invoked. As talked about that event afterward, the last thing he remembers thinking was that he was about to enter the home where the memories of his father would be impossible to avoid any longer.

The case of Russell is a good example of how engrained in a CDer's personality the avoidance of feeling becomes. Everything about who we are and how we act is modified in some way to avoid thoughts that evoke strong feelings.

The Taskmaster of Shame

Almost always there is a particular person in your life who was instrumental in teaching you to shame your feelings. For some it was a parent; for others it was a teacher or clergyman. Here is what others have told me about the people in their lives who taught them to be ashamed of their feelings:

Peter: "I'll never forget the day the priest scolded me for kissing a girl on the playground . . ."

Ann: "My mother told me only bad girls talked back to their parents and then she slapped me across the face, and even though I was furious at my mother for having humiliated me in front of the softball team, I never expressed my anger to her again."

Jenny: "I was really proud of my first painting, until I showed it to my brother who ran outside with it and made fun of it in front of his friends. By the time I came out to get it, they were all laughing hysterically at me."

John: "The assignment was to write an essay on something that was important to me. So I wrote a great essay on my dog. After I finished reading it to the class, there were lots of snickers and even the teacher seemed to be laughing at me."

As children, we protect the people we love. We don't want to think of them as doing harm to us, so we repress those memories or try to reinterpret them as "loving." For example, "Dad beat me because he loved me and didn't want me to grow up spoiled." Or, "Mom would humiliate me because she worried that I was making the same mistakes she made."

You suffered great pain at the hands of someone you believed truly loved you. An essential part of letting that pain go and relearning how to feel is to fully acknowledge what happened to you. Someone did you a grave disservice by shaming your feelings, regardless of what you think their motives may have been. It doesn't make that person evil, but even if they had the best of intentions, it doesn't erase the truth of what happened to you.

People who fear their feelings are threatened by others who don't fear their feelings. They feel compelled to control other people, especially children, and teach them to fear feelings by shaming them. It is a vicious cycle that perpetuates emotional shame from generation to generation. Aren't you ready to stop the cycle?

The following questions will help you pinpoint the ways in which your caregivers may have contributed to your chronic discontent. Take your time and answer each question honestly:

	YES	NO
1. Were you physically or sexually abused by a parent, caregiver, sibling, or other family member?		
2. Were you often verbally berated, blamed for family problems, or made to feel rejected?		

	YES	NO
3. Were your caregivers obsessively preoccupied with your life (e.g., friends, activities, feelings, etc.)?		
4. Did your caregivers become jealous when you formed other necessary and innocent relationships, such as a relationship with another family member or friend?		
5. Were you made to feel that your worth depended upon your accomplishments (e.g., making the football team, winning a scholarship, etc.)?		
6. Were you taught that certain feelings are wrong, and you should be ashamed for feeling them?		
7. Did you have the sense that your needs were always secondary to those of your caregivers?		
8. Was there a family hardship or trauma that made one of your caregivers emotionally unavailable to you?		
9. Would you categorize your relationship with your caregivers as more intellectual than emotional?		

If you answered "yes" to any of these questions, there's a good chance that your chronic discontent has firm roots in your childhood. As you read through the remainder of this chapter, you will begin to understand the specific ways in which your caregivers taught you to abandon your emotions.

There are some important ways in which your protective and loving connection with your parents may have been flawed and caused you to shut down the process of feeling as an adult. In the remainder of this chapter, we look at the five most common: extreme moral rigidity, physical or emotional abandonment, attacking, overprotectiveness, and triangulation.

Moral Rigidity

Leslie was the senior prom queen in high school. Although she's now in her mid-forties, her life is much like it was in high school; she always does the "right things." She's very active in her church—a past president of the women's circle—and is always busy with a fundraising project for some worthy cause. She married a very smart and ambitious man, Claude, who quickly became a successful urologist after medical school. Her three children are superstars, the oldest boy is now in high school and is the star athlete. The two younger girls are each excelling in academics and music respectively. From all appearances, Leslie's life is perfect.

Lately, however, there is a hard—almost bitter edge—to Leslie's personality. Friends and family have noticed that she's pleasant as long as things are going exactly as she planned, but is quick to anger if they aren't. Privately, Leslie has started seeing a therapist (she could never tell anyone that she was seeking help—after all, people might get the wrong idea) and a repeating theme in her therapy is that although she has everything she thought she wanted, she is unhappy, and can't figure out why.

Her therapist, skilled in treating chronic discontent, began to probe into her memories of childhood. Leslie didn't really see the need; after all, she had normal childhood in a loving family. She was certain there wasn't any trace of abuse in her past.

Leslie's mother had been a child of the Great Depression. She grew up very poor when her father lost the family business during the worst of the depression. As a young girl, Leslie's mother had been deeply ashamed of her family's poverty and was determined to pull herself into a higher social stratum just as soon as she could get out of the wood-frame house in the run-down neighborhood where she grew up.

When Leslie's mother had children, she was determined

that her children would never have to experience what she did. They would be educated, successful, and most importantly, have social status. She pushed Leslie, insisting that she make friends with other girls from "good" families.

Once in high school, Leslie accepted a date from a charming young man, Scott, who was raised by a single mother who was abandoned by her husband before Scott entered the first grade. Leslie's mother was furious with Leslie for accepting the date and insisted that she call Scott immediately and cancel. Why, if she were seen out with this young man, might people think she was of the same class?

Leslie's mother had established very strict rules for her family. Everything, including how to act in public, where they could dine out for dinner, what they could wear, etc. was regimented by her dictates.

Leslie knew from the time she was very young that she must marry a successful man. She knew she must never do anything that would embarrass her family publicly, and should always be accepted in the "right" crowd. There were so many rules, all unspoken but known very well to Leslie. Leslie's lot in life was to be perfect—or at least, "perfect" as her mother defined it.

Now in therapy, Leslie would often come to sessions and do nothing but cry the entire hour. "Why am I so ungrateful? I should be happy," she'd ask. Everything she'd worked so hard for didn't make her happy, and yet, she couldn't imagine doing things any differently. She'd done all the right things— those things that are supposed to make her happy, yet she was miserable. "What is wrong with me?" was a question she repeated often.

In the case of Leslie, her chronic discontent had strong roots in her mother's rigid rules about right and wrong. Leslie was never allowed to explore her options in life. Instead, she was handed a blueprint for her life on a silver platter. Her mother had the best of intentions of Leslie, no doubt wanting her to avoid the mistakes she and her parents had made. She was determined that what would make Leslie happy was to have all the right things.

What did Leslie do? Before she was even old enough to know the consequences of her actions, she learned to avoid her own feelings and do as she was told. After all, her mother loved her, and wanted the absolute best for her. Wasn't it her mother's support, after all, that made her so successful? How could that have been harmful?

But it was harmful. It taught Leslie the way of chronic discontent early in life. The messages were:

- "You don't know what's best for you. Your feelings will only get you into trouble."
- "This is for your own good. Be a good daughter and make me happy, too."
- "Happiness in life comes from what other people think of you."

Children who grow up in an environment where they are not allowed to deviate from a strict model of "good" behavior often find themselves battling chronic discontent.

"But I thought it was a good thing to instill a strong sense of right and wrong in children!" you say. On the surface, it does seem like a good thing to do.

The problem is that when a parent forces a child to accept unquestioningly a model of behavior and feelings, the child's own development is thwarted. The child can't feel what the parent wants her to feel, no matter how hard she tries. The child feels what she feels. When her feelings are belittled or condemned, she is left to only avoid those feelings in the future. Her parents cannot make her feel "desirable" feelings.

The natural course of development is for a child to feel her feelings and act on them. Sometimes, especially early in life, these feelings land the child in trouble. For example, when a young boy visits the store with his mother and wants the candy bar she has refused to buy him, he decides to act on his feelings and steal the candy bar when she's not looking. Once they are home, the mother discovers the child's stolen candy bar and then requires him to experience the consequences of his actions, namely to take the bar back to the store and apologize to the store manager. In the future, the child's feelings for the candy bar are changed. He may still want the bar, but knows he must pay for it if he really wants it.

The child who learns to reject his feelings refuses to consider the candy bar, because only bad boys want to eat a candy bar between meals. What has he learned? Not how to handle his feelings, but to deny his feelings as bad and unacceptable.

These may seem like insignificant distinctions, but to the child they make an enormous difference. He can either think: "If I really want the candy bar, then I must take my allowance to the checkout and buy it." Or, "I shouldn't want a candy bar. It's bad to eat sweets."

As an adult, the little boy can grow up and think "I will be an artist because I love making sculptures and am good at it." Or, he will think "I cannot be an artist. It is very hard to make a living from one's art. I should be something that makes me more financially secure." The pattern of learning to deny your feelings is often learned at an insidiously young age. Such patterns can shape your entire life into something that has very little resemblance to what you really want in life.

Because of the devastating effect of moral rigidity in childhood, children who grow up in dogmatic and fundamentalist religions of any sect or belief often discover themselves as adults struggling with chronic discontent. The rules of such religions often dictate that an individual's feelings are insignificant, and most teach that feelings are potentially evil.

But if we all followed our feelings, then the world would be one drunken orgy and nothing productive would happen, right? Having known many people who are strongly moral and very in touch with their feelings, I can confidently tell you that it isn't true. That's the way it seems to those of us with chronic discontent, but that's because we have no practice with handling our feelings, and they scare us. The view of the world out-of-control and drunk on feelings is projected view of our own fears and inability to handle our feelings. Had we grown up without chronic discontent, we would know that experiencing your feelings makes us strong, more secure in ourselves, and feeds our moral integrity.

Any child who is taught that his or her feelings are bad, is belittled for his feelings, or worse, punished for what he feels, is in danger of developing a life pattern of chronic discontent. Children (and adults) must learn to *handle* their feelings appropriately, not avoid them. The advocates of moral rigidity, whether they are parents, teachers, ministers, or rabbis, too often teach avoidance instead of coping.

Abandonment

John never knew the twins. They died a few years before he was born. In fact, very few people ever met the twins, as they were only six days old when they both died. Born too early in a time before medical science could save them, they succumbed to lungs that weren't developed enough to support their tiny bodies outside the womb.

All John remembers of the twins was spending occasional Saturday afternoons in the summer at their grave site, helping his parents plant flowers and tend to the lawn. He remembers his mother sometimes crying for no reason, and the beautiful, silver-carved frames that held their tiny newborn faces up on the mantle.

John describes his mother as kind, but distant. He felt that she loved him, but couldn't really remember her holding him or telling him so. She was depressed for much of his childhood, even being hospitalized at one point, and everyone in the family treated her as if she were very fragile. There was to be no crying, no complaining or whining, and no loud play in her presence. His father would remind him sternly: "Go to your room so your mother can have some peace and quiet."

John's father was preoccupied with caring for his mother for most of John's childhood. He had all he could handle—a demanding job, two children, and a wife who sometimes went days without leaving the bedroom. He cooked, cleaned, and shopped for the family when she couldn't. John was certain that his father dearly loved his mother, and thinks of him as nothing short of a living saint.

John grew up taking care of himself for the most part. He learned early to prepare his own breakfast and walk himself to school. When he was old enough to ride a bike, he took over the grocery shopping and eventually even cooked dinner a few nights a week.

As an adult, John suffers from chronic discontent. He is very responsible, has a loving family, but finds himself bored with life. Nothing he does really seems to mean much to him.

The roots of John's chronic discontent lie in the emotional

abandonment he experienced as a child. The difficulties his parents struggled through while he was a child left nothing for them to give to John. Their consuming grief over the loss of the twins and his mother's ongoing depression left them unavailable to the everyday scrapes and stories of a little boy. There was no harm intended here; they were simply trying to cope with their own problems.

As a result, John grew up too quickly. He learned to abandon his childhood feelings and be a good boy for his mother's sake. There was no time for his crying or complaints. He had to take care of himself and his mother. A sense of emotional responsibility for his mother replaced his own need to express his feelings.

John spent much of his adult life doing just what had helped him survive as a child: swallowing his feelings and getting on with life. He avoided any conflict, kept a clear focus on the practicalities of life, and always kept himself moving forward.

Now in his late thirties, John feels his life is like a hollow shell. All the pieces are there, but in his words "there's nothing there." John was an emotionally abandoned child who became an adult with chronic discontent.

Emotional abandonment can happen for many reasons. Children who are born to parents who are emotionally unavailable or who physically abandon them are two big reasons. Other causes for emotional abandonment can be too many siblings competing for the parents' attention or a family tragedy that consumes the parents' emotional energy during the child's young years. Whatever the cause, the result is the same: the child's emotional development is stunted. He or she is forced to function in an adult world without the benefit of those years where children normally have parents who help them learn how to properly handle their emotions. Left to fend for themselves too early, more often than not, the child learns the patterns of chronic discontent as a way of survival.

Children who were emotionally abandoned are often reluctant to confront this as an adult. They love their parents, and many believe that their parents did nothing wrong. Like John, they often put their parents on a pedestal for having to cope with such great difficulties in life. They often say things like, "She wanted to care for me and would have, had it not been for . . ." Or, "He couldn't help it. He was doing everything he could."

Emotional abandonment isn't defined by the intent of the caregiver—they often have the highest of intentions—it is defined by the effect on the child. Regardless of how well meaning they may have been, emotionally absent parents do not provide the environment that a child needs for healthy development. When the child is deprived of daily love, attention, and affection, the effects are damaging.

Were you emotionally abandoned as a child? Take a minute and seriously ask yourself these questions. What you know about your own childhood may amaze you!

1. Do you remember your parents telling you that they loved you? Hugging you? If so, how often?
2. Were you consistently afraid to tell your parents the truth about who you were are what you had done?
3. Did you often feel as if you were an inconvenience or that taking care of you was a chore for your parents?
4. Do you remember feeling that your parents were too busy or preoccupied to be concerned with what troubled you?
5. Did you often feel like an alien, a child who wasn't born to your parents but was dropped into your family from somewhere else?
6. Did you feel wanted as a child?

Take a minute and seriously think over your answers to these questions. If find any one of these questions brings back strong memories, that's good indication that you may have suffered emotional abandonment at a time in your development when you needed nurturing. To cope, it's quite possible that you learned the patterns withdrawal that now create chronic discontent in your life.

Attacking

Charlotte remembers the glass just missing her head and crashing into the wall behind her. In front of her stood her mother, calling her "trash" for having stayed out past midnight with her boyfriend. This wasn't the first time Charlotte's mother attacked her, but it was the last. Her boyfriend, who was just outside the door, came in, and grabbed her mother's hand just as she started slap Charlotte's face. "That," he growled, "is the last-time you'll ever lay a hand on her. We've decided to get married." He added tersely, "And if you ever want to see your daughter again, you had better stop now."

It was to be the last time Charlotte was attacked by her mother. She was married and moved out of the house several months later.

Charlotte's memories of abuse from her mother spanned her entire childhood. The fourth of six children, her mother had seemed to grow increasingly impatient with the younger children, ready to have all of them out of the house. Frequently, she reminded them of how much she had sacrificed to have them.

There were never any real bruises or broken bones—it wasn't that kind of abuse. But make no mistake, *it was abuse.* And it was a particularly damaging kind of abuse because it was never dramatic enough to garner the attention and protection of others. To many, it seemed like good, hard discipline.

- Charlotte remembers an argument she had with her mother over doing the laundry, and her mother becoming so enraged that she picked up the nine-year-old by her hair and shook her.
- Charlotte remembers being mocked by her father because she couldn't throw a ball. In exaggerated style, he imitated her at a family gathering until she ran inside crying from the embarrassment.
- Charlotte remembers her father becoming so angry with her that he would go outside, cut off a willow branch, and whip her until her legs had red streaks across them. She remembers how they would sting for hours afterward.
- Charlotte remembers making a surprise cake for her mother's birthday. When her mother came home, all she could say was that the kitchen was "such a mess."
- Charlotte remembers her mother picking up the telephone extension and gruffly telling her to "get off the phone right this minute" while she was talking to a friend from school.
- Charlotte remembers her mother hitting her on many different occasions and then telling Charlotte that it was her own fault because she was a bad girl.

All of this, to varying degrees, was abusive. Verbally, emotionally, and physically abusive. Even though it caused her great pain and distress, she never realized that it was abuse until years later. Only then was she able to look back at the pain of her childhood and acknowledge that much of it could have been avoided, if her parents had not been abusive.

Abuse from a trusted parent or caregiver forces a child to go inward with shame. She blames herself for what is happening to her and convinces herself that she is bad. She may begin to feel that there is a part of her self that is defective and can't be trusted. She learns to shame herself for her feelings and actions. The abuse drills shame into her psyche like no other experience can.

Childhood abuse can result in many things, but one of them is chronic discontent in adulthood. When the abused child learns to cope with the abuse by withdrawing and hiding her feelings, then she begins to develop the patterns of chronic discontent.

Many adults who were abused as children suffer from chronic discontent. Because most of their early memories of emotions were of being afraid, humiliated, or hurt, they quickly learned to avoid any feeling at all. They learned the primary technique of chronic discontent—turning off their ability to feel.

Overprotective

On the opposite side from attacking is the equally damaging practice of overprotecting a child. It happens when:

- The parent is hyper-vigilant; always looking for ways to protect the child from both real and imagined dangers.
- The parent intervenes in relationships where the child feels strong feelings (e.g., removes the child from a teacher who corrects the child or immediately reprimands the parents of other children who may be in conflict with the child).

The overprotected child is shielded from the natural shaping forces that help children to grow and develop. There is a certain amount of conflict and difficulty that every child must experience in order to grow up emotionally healthy. When a parent consistently intervenes and minimizes the experiences, the child is prevented from developing healthy coping skills.

Tatiana loved her children more than anything else in the world. A Russian immigrant who married an American citizen, she was widowed five years after having her second child, Rebecca. As her children grew into teenagers, she poured herself into her children's lives, doing everything she could to make their lives easier than hers had been as a poor farmer's daughter back in Russia.

Rebecca recalls how her mother would never allow her to walk the short three blocks home from school alone. Every day when the final bell rang, her mother would be waiting outside the classroom door to walk Rebecca home. She remember her mother double-checking her homework every night, and sometimes calling her teachers at home to discuss the assignment. Rebecca was only allowed to play with her friends while her mother was there to watch over them.

Once, Rebecca remembers a neighborhood boy riding his bicycle past her house. When he stopped to talk with Rebecca, her mother called to her from the window and told her it was time to come in. That was pretty much how it always was when a stranger came by.

As Rebecca entered high school, she showed remarkable scholastic ability and was at the top of her class. During her last semester as a junior, she found herself struggling with advanced calculus and ended the semester by earning a "B". When Rebecca brought that report card home, she remembers her mother flying into a rage at the teacher who had given Rebecca the B and immediately went back up to the high school to confront the teacher. Rebecca knew that she had been lucky to get even a B and had wished her mother would just stay out of it, but Tatiana insisted that her child could have only earned an "A". The teacher, so distraught and intimidated by the ranting Tatiana, agreed to give Rebecca some extra projects and if she performed well on them, to raise the grade to an A.

As an adult, Rebecca married shortly after finishing graduate school in biochemistry. In the decade that followed, her marriage fell apart as did a second marriage. She struggled to make friends and find some happiness, but now in her mid-thirties, she felt that she had been successful at neither.

Rebecca's chronic discontent finds its roots in her overprotected childhood. While her mother did everything for her from a heart of love, she inadvertently did damage to her young daughter. Rebecca needed to learn how to deal with conflict, failure, and hardship. Tatiana's overprotective love for her shielded her from these vital lessons.

More importantly, Tatiana's behavior toward her child communicated a very strong lesson: "Failure, rejection, and pain are unbearable. You must never feel them as I have." Subtly, she taught her child to fear her feelings. By labeling some as unbearable, she instilled a fear of all feelings. When Rebecca became an adult and no longer had her mother to protect her from these feelings, she had no skills for coping with feelings. To survive, she soon learned to do avoid feeling, and thus began her journey into chronic discontent.

Triangulation

The final source of childhood experiences that can develop into chronic discontent is *triangulation*. To understand this, just think of a triangle that is made up of a child, a mother, and a father. Triangulation occurs when one of the parents tries to use the child to manipulate the other parent.

When Beverly left the house for college, her parents separated and soon thereafter divorced. It was a big surprise to Beverly that they did it, but it was also a big relief. After years of sniping at one another, they had finally decided to go their separate ways. Beverly loved them both and hoped that each would finally find some happiness.

One of many memories that Beverly has of triangulation occurred during the walk she would take with her mother every evening after dinner. Since her mother suffered from a mild case of high blood pressure, the doctor had urged her to walk several miles a day to help control it without medication. Every night, like clockwork, Beverly and her mother would put away the last of the dinner dishes and then head out for a brisk walk about the neighborhood.

During those walks, Beverly remembers how her mother used to complain to Beverly about her father. Her mother would talk about how thoughtless her father had been and how he refused to stand up to his controlling father. She would grumble about his lack of business sense and how much money he'd lost in investments. She'd end every one of those conversations with something like: "Don't tell your father what I said. This is just between me and you."

Beverly remembers feeling torn, because she loved her father and looked forward to the weekends when they would spend both Saturday and Sunday together. They would fish, ride their horses, or maybe take the jeep out on some of the nearby 4-wheel-drive roads.

Beverly loved her mother, too, and often felt when she was spending time with one or the other of her parents, that she was letting the other one down. Particularly with her mother, she felt that her relationship with her father somehow hurt her mother's feelings.

Triangulation, like Beverly experienced, also occurs among some young children whose parents have divorced. When they are with one parent, they feel that they are somehow betraying the other parent. In some cases, one or both parents attempt to manipulate the other through the child. They might say things like:

- "Don't tell your father this, it would kill him."
- "Your mother is too strict with you."
- "Next time, ask me first. I'll handle your father."

Triangulation is a major disruption in the early cocoon of the parental relationship with child. It causes the child to learn to "disassociate" certain feelings for a parent when in the presence of the other parent. It's incredibly confusing to a young mind and often causes such distress that the child retreats and builds "a mental wall" between himself and his confusing feelings.

The message of triangulation is "you should feel a certain way about me and another way about your other parent." In adulthood, that message translates into separating one's self from his or her feelings, the first step into chronic discontent.

The Return of the Prodigal

Sometimes, we develop chronic discontent through our own devices, regardless of how we were parented. In this case, it is our own desire to be the "good" son or daughter that pushes us to deny feelings that might be disappointing to our loving parents. We desperately never want to become the kind of person that would disappoint them.

In the Bible, there is the very familiar story of the return of the prodigal son. In this story, we see a son who starts on a seeming independent, self-directed path, but who gives up his life in an attempt to return to the safety of his childhood home.

The story is of a son who demands his inheritance so he can leave home and see the world. Eventually, the father gives his son his inheritance and the son leaves home to see the world. After a few years of living largely, the son returns home penniless begging his father to take him back in. The father, overjoyed at the return of his son, welcomes him back, prepares a feast, and takes him back into the household. There is no doubt that the father deeply loves his son.

The prodigal son is a heartwarming tale that, contrary to conventional wisdom, says that you can go home again. But can you?

One of the most common beginnings of chronic discontent is found in this story. The son, obviously a curious and adventuresome fellow, wants to see the world. Symbolically, he is following his heart and throwing convention (and reason) to the wind, only to later return home beaten and defeated. The father genuinely loves his son and does what any loving father would do: he welcomes him back into the family.

The son has learned his lesson.

"I should never follow my heart—it will only lead to disaster."

"Better not to be curious."

"In the end, it would have been better if I had just accepted my father's ways and never ventured forth."

You can just imagine that the son never made the mistake of following his feelings again. He probably stayed on the farm and did the right thing. Out of his own heart, he wanted to please his generous and loving father.

But what kind of life did he have? The Bible doesn't tell us, but you need only to look around you to find out. This is the story of so many of us who at a young age strike out into the world to get married, move away, take a job, travel the world, live in a commune—you name it, for every generation has its unique way of leaving home. Then disaster strikes. Maybe the marriage falls apart and the daughter has a child to care for alone. Or the job falls through and the son has no way to make a living. Or travel money runs out and the commune wasn't what it seemed it would be. Then, the young adult goes back home in defeat.

The grown child so completely defeated and humiliated at not taking the earlier advice of his or her parents, resolves now to be "the good child." He or she takes on the values, dreams, and expectations of the parents and begins to live the life that is expected of him or her. That big defeat so early in life sent the child fleeing in retreat, back into the "safe" world of his or her childhood.

But what about the young adult child's dreams, hopes, and feelings—the very things that pushed him or her to leave home in the beginning? They are stuffed, swallowed, and locked tightly away. The child shames him or herself for those feelings and develops a great fear of making the mistake of following his or her feelings again.

No matter how we learned it, whether through our childhood experiences or from our own insatiable desire to be acceptable, the fact remains: we learned to shame ourselves for our true feelings. That shame may have begun deep in our past, but is alive and well in our lives today. The task before us is to face the shame, and in the process, begin to disempower it.

5

Excuse Me, Where's the Nearest Exit?

In the last chapter, we saw how shame develops in our lives. We also saw how it lives on and continues to affect our relationships, long after we have moved on in life. We also saw that the primary effect of shame is the avoidance of feelings and emotional withdrawal. By withdrawing from situations and relationships that evoke strong feelings within us, we also avoid the shame that demeans and punishes us.

Time to Run

Because people with chronic discontent tend to withdraw when things get too heavy, too sticky, in short, too emotional and because just about everything in life has periods of being too heavy, too sticky, and too emotional, we find ourselves eventually withdrawing from most everything that we do. Some things, like marriage and career, may be too difficult or expensive to physically withdraw from, so we emotionally withdraw from them. We show up, but our hearts aren't in it.

People with chronic discontent are professionals when it

comes to quitting. We do it all the time. The job, relationship, new project, hobby, friends, pets . . . we have quit them all. Why? Because they demanded too much from us emotionally. They threatened to leave us, made us feel like a failure, frustrated us, or made us feel inadequate. We started all of them with the best of intentions and lots of energy, but eventually we hit that too familiar emotional wall, and the price of getting past it was just too great. So we withdrew.

How have you withdrawn? Let's say you're a single woman and you meet another single man. He's handsome, caring, and seems to really like you after a few months of dating. Things are going well, and he wants to know if you love him. In fact, you suspect he may be preparing to ask you to marry him. What do you do? You test this idea by examining how you feel about him when you're with him.

How do you feel? More than likely you vacillate from feeling great to feeling vulnerable and silly. Your emotional shame kicks in and tells you that he'll probably leave you when he really gets to know you or that he'll be a jerk like all the other ones before him. Sometimes you get angry and irritable with him because you imagine the worst will happen to your relationship. How do you feel? You feel great on occasions and miserable on others.

This is where your withdrawal kicks in. You're scared out of your wits by these strong emotions, so you start unconsciously looking for an escape hatch. Maybe you:

- Start to fixate on some irritating habit or characteristic of his until it overwhelms any good thoughts you might have had about him
- Talk yourself out of the relationship by telling yourself (and all your friends) only the worst about him, omitting the positive.

- Begin to treat him miserably so that he eventually does leave you.
- Become emotionally distant and sexually cold.

Your conclusion? You don't love him, and you move on to the next relationship. Tragically, it was a relationship that might have been wonderful for you; instead you rejected it because you didn't feel good about it, mostly because you are scared of your own feelings.

There are several ways people with chronic discontent may choose to withdraw:

- Emotional Withdrawal
- Living Trances
- Destructive Intervention
- Instant Transformation

Emotional Withdrawal

Probably the most common and detrimental way that CDers withdraw is *emotional withdrawal.* It happens when you "quit and stay"; your body is still present, but your heart's not in it. You go through the motions, but you no longer care about what you are doing.

Emotional withdrawal can begin in our relationships whenever we sense those old, remembered feelings of shame overwhelming us. We may not be able to physically leave the relationship, for a variety of social, economic, or legal reasons, so we withdraw ourselves emotionally. We stay in the relationship, but we kill our passion and motivation for it.

Not a few marriages between CDers have lasted entire lifetimes with both parties emotionally withdrawn. To stay and talk about the differences, hurts, hopes, and needs is too painful. But leaving is much too painful. So we stay, and go through the motions.

Sandra and Greg have been married for 27 years. They are both working professionals; Sandra is a stockbroker and Greg is a partner in a law firm. On the outside, their lives are very comfortable and successful.

Many years ago, Greg had an affair with another woman. Sandra discovered the affair and rather than confronting Greg, she withdrew from him. Greg, sensing that Sandra knew the truth, terminated the affair. Since then, Sandra and Greg have lived a very routine existence. On weekdays they both work long hours, come home around 7 P.M. Sandra cooks dinner and Greg walks the dog and finishes the work he brought home. At around 9 P.M. they retire to the bedroom and read for awhile before falling asleep. For the last ten years, they haven't had sex at all.

Weekends are also well routinized. On Friday night they pack up the SUV with groceries and the dogs and drive up to their cabin in the nearby mountains. Saturday they work around the cabin, and then have dinner with friends who live nearby. On Sunday, they always go to the local market (in the summer they go to the local farmer's market) and buy groceries for the coming week. Around noon on Sunday, they pack up the SUV and head back home.

Sandra and Greg go through their marriage without evoking the powerful feelings of hurt, anger, and disappointment that are beneath the surface. By establishing routines, there is little need to talk about something that might elicit feelings. They both know the schedule and then follow it without question.

Of course, it's not that they don't communicate. They talk about what they did at work, what their friends are doing, or what they will buy at the market. What they don't talk about *ever* are their feelings.

For Sandra and Greg, so much time has gone by that it actually has become very difficult for either one of them to break through the emotional withdrawal. The festering feelings have been suppressed for so long, that both are afraid that any disruption in their predictable lives will create a crack in the dam that causes the whole marriage to collapse.

The Living Trance

One way of withdrawing from an emotionally charged situation or relationship is to throw yourself into an activity so deeply that you "lose yourself" in it. It's a kind of *trance* that you throw yourself into to avoid dealing with what is happening in your life at the moment. Let me share with you the story of a good friend of mine who used the trance of throwing herself into her job to avoid dealing with a marriage that was on the rocks.

Susan was a dear friend, and despite the fact that we rarely saw one another, when we got together, we always had a wonderful time. She was an attorney and had worked her way up the corporate ladder to become the vice president of human resources for a major corporation.

Earlier in her life, Susan had been a married housewife in California. When her husband ran off with another woman, Susan quickly found herself looking for a job to support her and her daughter. She went to work as a legal secretary and attended law school at night. After years of truly hard work, she graduated top of her class, and shortly thereafter, passed the California bar examination on her first try.

The memory of her failed marriage and the feelings of rejection and despondency never left Susan, despite the fact that she had pulled herself up and been very successful. She started work in the legal department at the company and was so successful in negotiating real estate contracts that she was quickly promoted up the ranks, eventually becoming head of the legal department. After ten years, her department was expanded to include the human resources department and she was given the title of senior vice president.

Fifteen years later, she fell in love with a man, Charles, who was a few years younger and much less successful than was she. She didn't mind at all, and was thrilled over the new relationship.

A year after they married, Charles became increasingly frustrated that Susan seemed to be distant and less attentive than she used to be. He began to feel like he had to make an appointment just to spend an evening alone with her.

Susan, extremely sensitive to the first signs of possible rejection, pulled back even more and poured herself into her job, regularly working 18-hour days. After another year, Charles began complaining that their relationship wasn't what it had been, and he insisted that they see a marriage counselor. Susan flatly refused, saying that they could solve their own problems. What Susan never told Charles, was that she had insisted in her first marriage that they go to counseling, and in counseling was when her ex-husband revealed that he was having an affair.

After another year of Susan completely submerging herself in her work through business trips that lasted for weeks and working late virtually every evening and on weekends, Charles moved out of their home and filed for divorce.

The tragic relationship of Susan and Charles is one that many people with chronic discontent have experienced in some form. The way that Susan numbed herself to the feelings of Charles' discontent was to create a trance of overwork rather than confront the issues and stay married to a man she loved. Sadly, her withdrawal only pushed Charles farther away and ultimately destroyed the marriage.

The trance of overwork is a perfect refuge for CDers in many ways. After all, who can criticize us for working so much? We can quickly blame it on the boss, the company, or the financial demands of our family. Our relationships outside of work may be falling apart, but we can effectively numb ourselves to the painful feelings with all the distractions, activity, and even stress of work.

Another common trance that people with chronic discontent use to lose themselves in is their family. Especially when our children are young and need a great deal of attention, it becomes easy to avoid our feelings by losing ourselves in the day-to-day activities of caring for them. There is so much to be done—buying the groceries, carpooling, parent-teacher conferences—we fall into bed exhausted at night. Then, at daybreak, it all starts again.

Year after year goes by, and we have numbed ourselves with all the activity of the family. Then suddenly, it all stops when the last child leaves home. What do you do then? Many CDers are caught in a tough place, having their favorite trance taken away, and they must find some other way of avoiding their own feelings. Maybe they go back to work, or start a rigorous schedule of volunteering or entertaining. Whatever they do, they must replace the trance or be forced to deal with their feelings. This is a terrifying thing, especially when you've effectively been able to avoid them for decades.

Destructive Intervention

One of the hardest things in life to acknowledge is that you have been your own worst enemy. Nobody likes to think that they have somehow deliberately sabotaged their own happiness; yet it happens all the time. I've done it, and so have you.

Destructive intervention happens when you withdraw by sabotaging your own happiness. It usually happens when you are afraid and are looking for an escape, but you can't find one. So, you begin sabotaging the situation. Let me explain this with an example:

For years, Beth wanted to be a caterer. Beth is a great cook and entertains in her home flawlessly, with seemingly little effort. Her dream was to one day quit her secretarial job and start her own catering business.

At one point, the company she worked for went through a tough economic period and was forced to lay off employees. The company was offering a generous severance package to anyone who chose to leave, so Beth decided to quit her job, take the severance pay, and start a catering business.

At first, times were tough, and she was barely able to break even. She paid close attention to every detail and made sure that each catering project was done to her highest standards. Sometimes, she would even lose money on a job because she refused to compromise with lower quality.

As the first year of catering came to close, her business still wasn't making much money. She made enough to pay for the food and the waiters, but there was hardly anything left over for her. She began to feel like a failure—a feeling that was full of shame and much self-deprecation. It was a feeling that was unbearable for Beth.

In first few months of her second year, Beth made a couple of big mistakes. First, an important job for the local chamber of commerce was completely botched. To start with, she forgot to place the order for the fresh shrimp (she needed far more than any of the local fish markets normally carried), so she was forced to substitute other dishes. Not only had she not ordered ahead of time, what she did prepare was little more than half of what was needed. The food ran out early in the evening, and soon thereafter, so did the wine. She tried to quickly send someone out to buy more, but it was too late. The manager of the chamber complained to her, and later refused to pay the bill. Not only did she lose the chamber's business but the mistake was very public, and she had several cancellations from other customers afterward. She began making other serious mistakes, and slowly her business diminished. After a year and a half, she closed the business and took another secretarial job.

Beth's experience with catering is a good example of how we sometimes use destructive intervention as a way of escaping feelings that are painful. By causing her catering business to fail, whether consciously or not, she was able to escape a situation that had become increasingly painful for her. So the catering business idea didn't work, after all. Who could blame her for trying?

Sometimes, like Beth, we unconsciously sabotage the situation as a means of escape. When the marriage isn't working, and we feel rejected and hurt, we have an affair with another person, which then completely destroys the marriage. Or, we forget our anniversary—five years running. Or, we become uncooperative, irritable, and unpleasant to be around.

Of course, we rarely can see it when we are deliberately sabotaging ourselves. Beth was convinced she was having a run of bad luck. When the marriage is failing, we are convinced that our partner just isn't trying hard enough. The list of reasons to which we ascribe our own shortcomings is often convincing and logical, hiding from view our own involvement in the sabotage.

Instant Transformation

Another of the favorite methods of withdrawal for CDers is "instant transformation." To put it simply, we make a U-turn and head in a new direction.

Katy was miserable at work. She was a paralegal for a large law firm, a job she had held since she graduated from college. The firm paid her well and gave her a great deal of autonomy to handle certain cases. Most of the time, there was little difference in her work and that of the junior attorneys at the firm.

Despite the objective reality of her job, Katy disliked it and found many reasons to find fault with it. She became increasingly frustrated with her boss and began to feel that she wasn't paid enough for the work she was doing. After all, she put out more work than some of the attorneys in the firm. "So what if I don't have a law degree?" she thought. "What counts is the work, and I do more than my share of it."

One day, Katy came in and surprised everyone by quitting. She felt that trying to work things out in the job was futile, and that she would be better off somewhere else. So she left the job where she had established herself and earned a great deal of respect, to start over as a dental assistant.

Other ways people with chronic discontent might try to instantly transform include:

- Buying a new house
- Buying a new car
- Becoming obsessed with a new hobby
- Having a baby

People with chronic discontent often convince ourselves that a situation is hopeless, and so we make a dramatic change in an effort to improve it. In many of these situations, things really aren't hopeless at all, *it is our resistance to dealing with our own feelings that is pushing us to withdraw.* We can't tolerate what we are feeling, so we run away. We start a new marriage. We go back to school and start a new career. We drop an old friend and move on to a new acquaintance.

Are you beginning to see how withdrawal works? It invades not only just your feelings, but the way you live your life. You begin to feel badly about virtually everything you try. Relationships almost always end up either fizzling out or with hurt feelings. You quit most jobs because you reached the point of feeling they were intolerable. Even hobbies and pastimes are dropped, as you almost always grow bored or frustrated with them.

- You bought a sewing machine and started making clothes . . . now it sits in the corner unused.
- You bought the woodworking equipment so you could make furniture on the weekends . . . now it sits dusty in the garage.
- You joined the gym determined to start a regular routine of exercise . . . now you can't remember the last time you went to the gym.

Of course, there's nothing wrong in trying something new and discovering you don't care for it, but it's different for CDers. *Everything* we try seems to eventually fade into boredom or disappointment.

It's definitely not that we don't try. In fact, we try harder than other people to find something that makes us happy. It's just that no matter what we try, even when we start out feeling a little jolt of excitement, it eventually poops out.

It's About "Showing Up"

The long-term effects of withdrawal are eroding your confidence and self-esteem. Every time you withdraw to avoid your feelings, you inadvertently create feelings of disappointment. In time, you convince yourself that you just can't have a good relationship or that every job eventually turns out to be drudgery.

If only we stayed engaged longer, we might discover that relationships can be worked to our satisfaction and that every job might have its low points, but also its triumphs.

There's a saying that is: "To finish first, you must first finish." You can't succeed at something once you've quit. You've got to stay engaged if you want the satisfaction of completion and success. Those of us with chronic discontent rarely stay engaged long enough to experience this, and no matter how close we come to success, once we withdraw, we are left with nothing but feelings of disappointment and frustration.

Once I heard some advice on the radio and it really shook my world. It's rare that something so simple brings so much insight, but this did for me. The speaker (I forget who it was) said "that the majority of success in life is about showing up." Maybe that doesn't hit you the way it did me, but it helped me realize that because I withdrew so often, I was missing out on many of the rewards of life.

I looked around at the people I knew who were successful. Most of them weren't brilliant or any better qualified than was I. It's simply that they *consistently showed up*. They were there, day in and day out. They weathered the storms, and in time, they reaped wonderful rewards for the effort.

If I looked at successful people whose careers I had known for years, their success was almost always because they stuck "with the knitting" through the hard times. If I looked at long-lasting relationships that I admired, the relationship worked because both people stuck with it through the difficult times. Success at the things that mattered in life really did depend on consistently showing up.

Because of my own chronic discontent, I was constantly on the move. I worked hard—in fact, very hard; but eventually something would happen that evoked those old feelings of shame and I would find a reason to withdraw. Those reasons made perfect sense on the surface, but the real issue was my chronic discontent. As time went by, I saw other people getting what they wanted out of life—a wonderful marriage, a successful and happy career, great friendships. What did I have? I had little bit of all of it, but not what I wanted. I had withdrawn too many times to build the life of my dreams.

This is one of the most important lessons you can learn from this book: *A lifetime of withdrawal cheats you of the life you want.* If you don't stay with it, don't persevere through the hard times and stay emotionally present, you can't create a fulfilling life.

A Cynic Is Born

When you have lived with this kind of continuous withdrawal and disappointment, you begin to expect that things just aren't going to work out. You expect the worst to happen. The voice in your head always gravitates to the negative possibilities.

Sara wanted to do something more for her family, now that the children were in school. She didn't feel comfortable taking a full-time job, so she decided to start a business in her home doing secretarial work. She had a computer, printer, and a few business contacts from the job she held before the kids were born.

The only problem was that Sara couldn't seem to sell her services. Every time she'd work up the courage to make a sales call to an office, she'd be convinced that they didn't need her services or that they'd think she couldn't handle the work. After all, she had spent the last ten years changing diapers and cooking meals. Maybe she didn't have what it took to get back into the fast pace of the business world.

Those automatic thoughts happened so quick for her, that she wasn't aware of how busy she was convincing herself that she couldn't get the work. The first time a potential client would inquire about her skill or her other clients, she'd fumble about and eventually leave without any success. Time and again this happened, until she finally gave up on starting the business. "Of course," she thought "these things never work out for me."

Sara is like so many with chronic discontent—she automatically expects for things to go badly. She hears all the reasons, over and over in her head like, why it is that she won't succeed and why it is unlikely that anyone could use her services. Because of this, her outward reaction to others is usually defensive. "What did he mean by that question?" Or, "Why is she smiling like that . . . is she making fun of me?"

This kind of reaction often creates the very result you imagine. Your defensive reactions don't inspire others to work with you. Or, you start out on a project with gusto, but because you convince yourself that it will likely fail, you don't follow through.

Those of us with chronic discontent do just like Sara in all areas of our lives. We imagine that our spouse is cheating on us, so we become distant and accusing—hardly the kind of person another wants to come home to. Or, we expect that something terrible has happened to our child, and we become overprotective parents that push the child to rebel against our strict rules. In so many ways, our negative expectations create the very situation that we don't want.

Looking for Others' Failures, Too

After living with this cycle of disappointment we grow increasingly more cynical about our life and the lives of those around us. We expect disappointment and just naturally look for it in everything and everyone around us.

- At the wedding of a good friend's daughter, we privately wonder how long it will be before the marriage falls apart.
- When an old friend calls whom we haven't heard from in years, we wonder what it is that he wants from us.
- When someone offers to do us a favor, we look for what they are really trying to get from us.

In order to make ourselves feel less crazy, we are compelled to look for the bad apple in everyone else's basket. When we find it, we're relieved to know that we're not so odd after all. If we are mostly frustrated, then aren't most people frustrated, too? And if they're not, isn't there something wrong with them?

Diane remembers how she used to use the prayer meeting at her church to make herself feel better. She would go and listen to all the prayer requests everyone in group would mention, things like: a son who was getting a divorce, an aunt who was dying of cancer, or a friend whose husband had lost his job. It wasn't that she had some macabre joy in other people's suffering; it was simply confirmation to her that everyone else's life was as difficult as her own.

Diane also noticed something that she used to do that is also very common among people with chronic discontent. Whenever she would get together with her friends, she would steer the conversation around to "ain't it awful" topics. Inevitably, it would be about how so-and-so's children were the terror of the neighborhood, or how so-and-so just refused to see that her husband was having an affair.

Let's Share the Misery

The relationships that people with chronic discontent develop are usually relationships that are based on a common complaint. For example, I know many struggling writers whose only friendships are based on the common complaints about the publishing business (advances are too small, editors don't "get" their book ideas, literary agents won't return their calls, etc.). When these writers get together, the bond of their friendship flows along the dimensions of their common discontent.

Maybe some of your friendships at work are based on your common dislike of the boss/company. Maybe your political affiliations are based solely on your dislike of a particular candidate or party. Often, people with discontent organize their lives around their favorite complaints onto which they focus their frustration and disappointment.

Barbara lives in a small community in west Texas. The land where her small farm sits is very dry and completely dependent upon the small stream that flows through her land. All of her water, including that in her home, is pumped out of the stream.

Many years ago, a doctor from a large city came to the area

and bought a large horse ranch just up the stream from Barbara's community. For admittedly selfish reasons, he allowed his horses to trample part of the stream that followed through his property, which meant that the horses inevitably defecated in or near the stream making the water downstream polluted and undrinkable.

After several angry confrontations with the doctor, Barbara organized her neighbors in a lawsuit against the doctor. The suit cost a great deal of money, and Barbara dedicated herself to raising the funds in any way she could. For almost ten years, Barbara was totally consumed with her mission against the doctor.

Even the though the doctor begrudgingly made changes to protect the stream, Barbara refused to give up her fight, eventually taking the lawsuit to the supreme court of the state. As the years dragged on, the issue seem to become more about Barbara's anger toward the doctor than it was about the stream.

Once the lawsuit was finally ended, Barbara then turned her attention toward unseating an elected judge of a lower court who had ruled against her early in the case. She successfully and almost single-handedly waged a campaign against the judge who then lost the election.

The story of Barbara tells us something very important about chronic discontent. It wasn't that Barbara was wrong to sue the doctor or to campaign against the judge. In the court of ethics, perhaps she was more than justified to do both. The issue is that she became possessed by her frustration and disappointment and organized her life around it. As soon as the lawsuit was finished, she needed something else to be angry about to fill the void. People like Barbara often move from cause to cause, always in search of a target for their chronic discontent.

You're Either My Friend or My Enemy

Another pattern of relationships for people with chronic discontent is that of seeing other people as either our friends or our enemies with no middle ground. In other words, if you're not working for us, then you're against us.

This attitude develops because our capacity for frustration and ambiguity is already stretched as far as it can go. We demand support and encouragement from our friends. Anything less, is assumed to be criticism—something for which we have little patience or tolerance.

Friendships sometimes end over seemingly insignificant events that we interpret as statements of no-support for our current cause. They failed to attend a party that we invited them to, so we assume they intended some statement of disapproval or criticism by their absence. Or, they seem uninterested in hearing the stories of our vacation to Hawaii, so we assume they think our vacation was inferior to their own vacation to Australia. Whatever the situation, people with chronic discontent have a strong tendency to ascribe evil intentions in the absence of expressions of approval or support.

Mike had decided that he needed a break from work and was going to take a three-week vacation of motorcycling around the country. One Saturday afternoon, he told his good friend George the plans for his vacation. George was skeptical about such a trip and asked him if he'd really thought about what it would be like to cross Nevada in the middle of summer or what he might do if it rained during his trip. Mike quietly grew angry with George's questions, but didn't show it. When George left late that afternoon, Mike decided that George was jealous of his idea (George had two small children and couldn't possibly take such a vacation himself), and that

George was trying to spoil his excitement. Rather than consider the issues George raised, Mike became even more determined to make the trip and from that point on made a point of not discussing it with George.

In a case like that of George and Mike, you can insert just about any set of circumstances and names, and come up with a scenario that's probably repeated many times in your life. Because people with chronic discontent live in a world of disappointment, our tolerance for criticism, however well intentioned and carefully delivered it may be, is very low. If a person makes the mistake of criticizing us too often, we usually end the relationship by withdrawing from it.

Because we're generally uncomfortable with the emotional expression that often accompanies confrontation, we rarely confront a friend who we perceive has transgressed our limits. To confront is far too risky, so instead we choose to withdraw and let the relationship die a slow and silent death.

This kind of "stealth" withdrawal often baffles those around us. It may take months or even years before they realize that we have ended our relationship with them—and what's more, they may not have a clue as to what caused the split. We usually avoid trading harsh words and will "go through the motions" of the relationship for a while as we grow increasingly distant.

Karen is an artist who has channeled some of her chronic discontent into her paintings. The finished canvases are usually minimal with a rather dark, almost foreboding scene. Over the 20 years since she graduated from art school, Karen has made her living from her artwork. During that time, she has signed on with several galleries around the country that sell her work. All in all, Karen is a successful artist.

Through the years, Karen has surrounded herself with friends and gallery owners who unquestioningly support her work. They never say anything critical, and are always praising her for her creativity and mastery of the craft.

It took Karen many years of showing in more than a dozen galleries to create such a network of support. In the early years, she would sign on with a gallery and if the gallery didn't show-case her work prominently or offered some critical feedback about her paintings, she would slowly stop sending the gallery paintings. Eventually, she would drop the gallery and move on to a gallery that she thought would be more supportive.

Obviously, it makes no sense for Karen to show her paint-ings in a gallery that doesn't believe in her work, but there is something more going on here. Karen couldn't tolerate feed-back of any kind, even feedback that could have made her much more successful. Instead, she needed to have unques-tioning approval from the galleries. As with her galleries, so it was with her friendships. Friends who admired her work and bought paintings from time to time were, in her mind, true friends. Other friends, who enjoyed her company but perhaps weren't wild about her art, were jettisoned.

Those of us who struggle with chronic discontent are highly susceptible to surrounding ourselves with only "yes-men." This may seem perfectly harmless when it comes to friendships, but in other relationships it can be quite detri-mental. As we slowly spin farther and farther away from real-ity, we have no one around us to gently guide us back on course. All of us need this from time to time, but because those of us with chronic discontent can't tolerate criticism, others know better than to offer it.

Where does this end? You and I have both seen where this goes, although we may not have recognized it at times. How often have you encountered an older relative, family friend, church member, or coworker who is bitter, has few or no friends, and complains about everything? That's where chronic discontent will take you if you let it. Chronic discontent eventually alienates you from other people. Nobody is perfect, and even though others love you dearly, they may need to offer some helpful feedback or disagree with you from time to time. The longer you refuse to tolerate such help, the more isolated you become.

6

The Comeback Kid

The art of the comeback—it's the art of people with chronic discontent. We know it so well; we've spent much our adult lives withdrawing and then trying to make a "comeback." It seems we're always trying to resurrect some area of our lives—starting a new relationship after a previous one failed, starting a new job after that last one drove us crazy, or starting a new hobby because we lost interest in the last one (and the one before that, too). We're always bouncing back from something.

That's our most endearing quality. Everyone cheers for the underdog, and in some aspect, it seems the person with chronic discontent is always the underdog. It's one of our strengths.

And one of our weaknesses, too. Every time we have to pull ourselves up, dust off, and start over again, it takes a little more out of us than it did before. Every comeback wears on us and drains just a little more of our precious energy. Comebacks are costly.

How many times can you find the inspiration, motivation and finances to start another new business after the previous one failed?

How many times can you fall in love only to have it fall apart, and still believe in the power of love?

Carolyn grew up in a small Midwestern town. Her parents were kind and hardworking. They had five children, and both of them had to work full-time jobs to pay the bills. Carolyn was the oldest child, so she had been the one at home who tended to the younger children while their mother was at work.

Carolyn's lifelong dream was to be nurse. After high school, she moved to the nearest larger town with a university and enrolled in the nursing program. With the combination of scholarships and a few part-time jobs along the way, she finished her nursing degree in four years and immediately went to work in one of the local hospitals.

Carolyn dated some in college, but the demands of nursing school consumed most of her time and energy. She was determined to get her degree, so she put romance on the back burner for a while. After school, she dated on occasion, but didn't seem to meet many men that were eligible.

Five years or so after graduating, Carolyn had become disenchanted with nursing. It just wasn't what she thought it would be. There was too much paperwork and not enough time to tend to patients. The pressures of managed care and hospital management were driving her to frustration and made her wonder just why she ever went into nursing.

She started back to night school to work on an MBA. It took her fives years and lots of hard work—juggling a full-time career and going back to college. The course material was very challenging for her, since she hadn't studied business before, but after many study groups and all-night cram sessions, she finally earned the degree.

The hospital where she worked wanted to promote her into

nursing management, but Carolyn felt she was ready to move on to something new, so she took a job as a production supervisor at a local glass plant. The hours were 9 to 5, unlike the shift-work of nursing, and the pay was much better.

She liked the job, although she soon discovered that the work was monotonous. The same reports had to be written. The same budget plans had to be completed. Everything seemed fairly regimented and routine. But this time, having spent so much time and effort earning the MBA, she was determined to stick with the job.

A few years after starting at the plant, the economy took a dive and layoffs at the plant were imminent. Although Carolyn had a great relationship with her boss, he told her that he might have to let her go. She was one of the most recent hires, and the layoff policy was "last hired, first fired." A year later, times got worse, and eventually the bad news came. Carolyn was out of work.

She had some savings that she could live off, while she tried to find other work. A local insurance company was hiring nurses as claims adjusters and they called to see if she was interested. Still sour on the idea of managed care, Carolyn didn't really like the idea of doing the job, but decided to take it. Who knew if anything else would be available?

For seven years, Carolyn grinded away at the insurance job. She hated the fact that she had become the very person that she despised when she worked at the hospital. She was now the contact person at the insurance company who approved or denied claims. Before any medical procedure could be done, it had to be approved by Carolyn if the insurance company was going to pay for it.

Although it had been years now since she worked in the hospital, she began to see those times in a different light. After working at the glass plant and for the insurance company, she had realized that being a hospital nurse was probably the best job she had held. But what could she do now?

She was in constant contact with the hospital because of her position at the insurance company, and she began to put "feelers" out about returning to hospital work. It had been over a decade since she had worked in a hospital. She wasn't even sure if she still remembered how to do the most routine tasks, like starting an IV transfusion or reading an X-ray. Could she still cut it in a hospital?

It took time and pulling lots of strings, but eventually the hospital hired her back into an entry-level nursing position. She was thrilled to be back, but also nervous about her ability to handle the job.

A few years went by, and Carolyn was promoted to head nurse for the surgery floor. The work was mainly administrative, not unlike her job at the glass plant, but she stuck with it. Somewhat defeated and discouraged, she resigned herself to being a hospital nurse for the rest of her career. It seemed to her that no matter what job she did, sooner or later, she was unhappy with it. Besides, she just didn't have the energy to start another new career.

Like Carolyn, each comeback drains you a little more than the one before. You start out with enthusiasm, pulling yourself up by the bootstraps, but then the discouragement slowly settles in, and you're back in the same place of discontent. Eventually, you just settle for what you have, and decide it will never be any better. After all, you tried, and every time you got the same results.

Every failed comeback destroys a little bit more of your hope for the future. If you withdrew and never tried again, you might still hope that things will one day be different. But you didn't do that. You pulled yourself up by your bootstraps, and marshaled all your resources. You were very courageous, reaching deep inside yourself to find the inspiration to start again. No one can (or should) ever say that you didn't try. God knows, you've worked at it harder than most everyone else you know.

That's why the disappointment that followed the withdrawal was so devastating. It's like you gambled all the passion and inspiration you own to make this happen, and when it fell apart, you were left with an empty heart.

This is the story of chronic discontent that most people don't know. It's story about true grit and determination. It's a story about having walked the high wire without an emotional net. It's about trusting, when a small voice in you tells you that you'll only be hurt again.

How many times can a person start over again? How many times can you give your heart away? How many times can you ignore the doubts and believe in yourself anyway? Each time you do it, it is harder. With each comeback, hope wanes just a bit more than before.

When CDers finally reach the point of having no more energy to comeback, they slip into something more serious: major depression. Major depression can take several forms, but the essence is a pervasive feeling of despair and hopelessness that paralyzes your mind. Life becomes a burden; and you have no hope that it will ever get any better.

This is the tragic point that most people with chronic discontent enter a psychotherapist's office. Major depression is a serious illness and psychotherapists are trained to spot the signs and offer treatment. The prognosis of overcoming major depression is very good if you get help, and less so if you do not. If you find yourself at the point of having no more comebacks left, I urge you to talk to a professional. There is help, and there's nothing good that come from denying yourself the help you need.

Treating major depression, however, often does nothing for the underlying chronic discontent. The savvy professional may diagnosis the situation as "double depression" (meaning major depressive episode in combination with dysthymia), but the treatments that are offered are typically aimed at relieving the major depression. Most clients feel so relieved after the major depressions lifts, that they terminate treatment and return to their life as it was. The problem is that the cause and symptoms of chronic discontent remain untreated. That's why the statistics bear out one painful fact: people with chronic discontent are more likely than others to experience major depression, and those who experience one period of major depression are far more likely to experience another episode than someone who never has. In other words, if you fail to work on the root cause of your chronic discontent, you're living on a very slippery slope that most likely won't get better, and will probably get worse.

I remember my first experiences of working with clients in graduate school. Frankly, the school always gave students the cases with the worst prognoses under the assumption that we probably couldn't do much harm.

I remember sitting across from clients who would tell me the most courageous life stories. Such courage I had never been forced to find within myself in those early years and I marveled at how they had survived some unbelievable circumstances. The fact that they were still able to function at all was a marvel.

Very often the first 20 or 30 years of their lives were spent pulling themselves up after tragedy. Just as soon as things started to look better again, some other tragedy would hit, knocking them down and forcing them to crawl back into the world the rest of us took for granted. By the time they were in mid-life, it seemed their ability to pull themselves back up had completely run out. There wasn't anything left. Hope had run dry.

I learned then a powerful lesson about life: *Hope is all that stands between us and insanity.*

Hope is fragile and precious. Each of us only gets so much of it in this lifetime, and once it is all spent, it is truly difficult to get back. Hope seems to create more hope, and conversely, when there is no hope left, there is no more to be had without some professional help.

The serious risk of the withdrawal-and-comeback cycle of chronic discontent is the loss of hope. As the years go on and the repeated withdrawals bring disappointment after disappointment, your supply of hope dwindles. Life diminishes from Technicolor to black and white to slow motion, and in some cases, to insufferable darkness.

You can do something to stop this undermining influence of chronic discontent. You can make a difference. It's difficult, painful, and frightening at times to do the work required, but it is worth it. If you stick with it, you can break the cycle.

One more comeback won't fix you. That's what we often tell ourselves: "This time it will work, and I will finally be happy." But it's not true. As long as you persist in the patterns of chronic discontent, this comeback will fail as have all the ones before.

In a few more chapters, we will begin to start the process of working on your chronic discontent. There are just a few more issues we need to discuss before we get to that, but as you continue reading begin to think about your own desire to leave chronic discontent behind in your life. Ask yourself if you're ready, and if you are, commit to doing what it takes. Everything you need is either in this book, or just one phone call away to a trained professional.

It all boils down to one thing. Are you committed to changing your life?

PART II

Chronic Discontent and You
(How's It Shaping Your Life?)

In the first section of this book, we learned the basics about chronic discontent:

- *At the core of chronic discontent, we've learned, is the shame we feel for our feelings. We hide, manipulate, and avoid feelings in order to avoid the punishing shame that we've associated with feelings.*
- *Feelings emerge primarily from our thoughts about relationships.*
- *Primary feelings occur in the present moment and are connected to what is happening right now.*
- *Remembered feelings are remnants of past relationships. Remembered feelings can interfere with our ability to feel primary feelings in the "now" moment.*
- *The most troublesome of all remembered feelings is shame.*
- *We avoid feelings primarily through avoidance and withdrawal.*
- *All forms of withdrawal, particularly emotional withdrawal, are damaging to the relationships we need to be content and fulfilled.*

- *Lifelong patterns of withdrawal create an ever-deepening sense of frustration, disappointment, and eventually despair.*
- *Chronic discontent leaves a deep imprint on our thinking, particularly in certain beliefs about life and relationships.*

In this section, we take what we've learned so far and see how it may be affecting you. In these chapters we look at the kinds of withdrawal games, beliefs, relationships, and remembered feelings that are specific to you. At the beginning of each chapter is a brief quiz to help you zero on the specific ways chronic discontent is shaping your life.

7

Withdrawal Games

(How Do You Play?)

The practice of emotional withdrawal evolves over time. When we are young, we simply throw a fit, pout, and stomp off to our rooms. As we grow older, our methods of withdrawal become more clever and complicated.

Adult methods of withdrawal are complicated because we know that *we can't appear to be withdrawing.* So, we must cleverly hide the fact that we are withdrawing from a relationship behind some more legitimate appearing reason. These kinds of complicated behaviors where an ulterior motive is being concealed are called games.

Everyone plays games, but people with chronic discontent play a particular kind of game that allows us to emotionally withdraw. Let me illustrate this with a simple, childhood game of withdrawal: a child might attempt to withdraw from school by complaining of a stomachache on test days. The "stomachache" provides the legitimizing reason for withdrawing and covers up the real reason for the withdrawal which the parents wouldn't likely accept, namely that the child is anxious about taking tests. Likewise, CDers play games that give us a "cover" story for withdrawing.

In this chapter, I've assembled some of the more popular games that people with chronic discontent play. Some of these games are ones that I've played many times to withdraw from relationships and some are games other CDers have told me about. While it is unlikely that you play all these games or that you play each game exactly as I describe it, it is very likely that you play many of these games in some variation or combination.

Here's a quiz that will show you which of the withdrawal games you play. Remember, be honest and don't spend too much time on any one question. Give the first answer that comes to mind.

Withdrawal Games Quiz

	YES	NO
1. I can't seem to find a place where people "get" me.		
2. I often wish that I lived somewhere else.		
3. I've tried many different careers.		
4. I never find much fulfillment in my work.		
5. Other people are often hurtful.		
6. If my family/friends were more attentive and loving toward me, I would be happier.		
7. Sometimes I buy things to cheer myself up.		
8. I owe more on credit cards than I can pay off in the near future.		
9. If it weren't for a particular tragedy in my past, I would be happy.		
10. I am basically flawed.		
11. Small things about other people often get on my nerves.		
12. I can't seem to meet nice people.		

	YES	NO
13. I pride myself in being difficult for other people to "read."		
14. My friends have no idea what I am feeling.		
15. My closest relationships have involved sex at one time or another.		
16. I have, on occasion, used sex to get what I want.		

SCORING

The items that you answered "yes" are associated with one of the withdrawal games you play. Look over the quiz and for any item that you answered "yes," find the associated game in the table below.

Items	Game
1–2	Geographic game
3–4	Career switch game
5–6	Emotional blame game
7–8	Debtor game
9–10	Wooden leg game
11–12	Blemish game
13–14	"Don't tell me what I'm feeling" game
15–16	Sexual game

The Geographic Game

"I hate this town—it's so backward."

"Nobody here understands me."

"Things will be different in _____."

You've heard people say these things before. Maybe you've

even said them yourself? The geographic game is all about withdrawing by moving to a new location. The game is played by first convincing yourself (and others) that the place where you now live is the source of your unhappiness and frustration. Then you tell yourself that life will be different in some other location. Finally, you pull out the moving boxes, pack up your possessions and start a new life somewhere else.

For a while, the geographic game seems to work. You're excited to be in a new place and making new friends. Life seems fresh and exhilarating again. Then, slowly the old frustrations and discontent comes back. In time, the glamour of the new place fades into new complaints.

I once heard Wayne Dyer tell about an encounter he once had after having appeared on *The Tonight Show*. Wayne lives in South Florida, and after his appearance on the show which is taped in the early afternoons, he flew back to Florida and was walking on the beach the next morning after the show aired. On the beach, he encountered a woman who had seen him the night before on television. She was surprised to see him there, as she couldn't figure out how he had made it down to Florida so quickly. Wayne explained that he lived in Florida, and had returned home after the taping of the show in the afternoon.

The woman told Wayne that she was thinking of moving to Florida, too. "How are the people down here?" she asked. Wayne answered with another question: "How are the people where you are from?"

The woman mentioned that the people where she was from were very busy and often rude. "Well," he said, "people are pretty much the same way here."

Further down the beach, he encountered a couple who had also seen him on television and mentioned that they were considering moving to Florida, too. They asked him "How are the people down here?" Wayne responded with the same question: "How are the people where you are from?" The couple replied that people where they were from were very friendly and outgoing. Again, Wayne responded, "People are pretty much the same way here."

The point that Wayne was making is that no matter where you live, you perceive the world around you the same. If you are discontent in your current location, no matter how snowy, rural, or impoverished it might be, you will likely be discontent in a sunny paradise where life is simple and easy. Discontent isn't associated with where you live—it is about how you feel. Changing your latitude won't change your feelings.

A good friend of mine had a mother who was discontent for most of her adult life. When her husband retired from work, they moved to Florida for retirement. Within a few years, they moved back to Alabama because they thought the people in Florida weren't very friendly. Then they moved to Colorado, but moved back in a few years because the winters in Colorado were too cold. Then they moved into a planned retirement community, but soon found themselves frustrated with all the structured activities. Then they moved into a house just down the street from where they had lived much of their married life where they stayed until eventually both of them passed away.

Because some of us with chronic discontent can't just pick up and leave our jobs or our children's schools, we stay in the same location, but blame all of our frustrations on the location. We tell ourselves that the minute we retire and the kids are out of college, we'll move to a better place. Tragically, a better place doesn't exist as long as we are under the influence of chronic discontent.

The Career Switch Game

When I was a young man, a well-meaning person once told me: "Alan, choose a career where you can make lots of money because no matter what career you choose, within five years you will be bored with it." The person who told me this was an older gentleman who had at different times in his life been a lawyer, a psychologist, a musician, and a journalist. Not one of those careers had really made him happy, so he concluded that fulfillment wasn't to be found in work.

Like the geographic game, the career switch games works on the same principle of blaming all your ills on your career. If only teachers were paid more, if the students were more committed, if the school board invested more in textbooks, then teaching would be a great job. Or, if only the company wasn't so profit-driven or if management cared about employees, then this would be a great job.

Because we spend the majority of our waking hours at work, the job becomes an easy target for all our frustrations and disappointments. Certainly, every job has its frustrations, so we capitalize upon those and add on top the long list of our own frustrations.

Job-hopping, even when each successive position is a promotion, is often a sign of chronic discontent. The boss was a jerk or the pay wasn't enough—the list of complaints can be as long as you can imagine. Every job eventually gets too frustrating and we move on, telling ourselves that the next one will be better. Or, it will be better when finally get a management position. Or, it will be better when we can run our own company. Despite what you may think, there are just as many discontented CEOs as there are discontent mailroom workers. I know because I've worked with many of both.

Sometimes the career switch leads people to make dramatic changes in their careers, like leaving a long-term position to become a consultant or writer. Self-employment for many CDers seems to hold the promise of escape from discontent. Unfortunately, what isn't apparent at the beginning is that self-employment may be free of the tyrannical boss, but the hassles of making a business financially viable more than replace it.

The Emotional Blame Game

"How am I? What do you care? My own daughter never calls me, and I sit here alone."

"If it weren't for you, I'd be happy."

"After all I've had to put up with you!"

This is the language of emotional blame. The essence of the game is to hold other person responsible for our bad feelings. Quite simply, it allows us to blame the other person for our withdrawal from the relationship. It is as if we say: "You make me feel badly, so I'm backing away from you."

One of the more tragic consequences of chronic discontent is the outcome of the emotional blame game: *We often blame the people most important to us for our painful feelings.* It's a very tragic game that often ends with us losing the people that mean the most to us.

Christine and Todd landed in marriage counseling after a tumultuous ten-year marriage. During their marriage, Todd had changed jobs six times, and they had moved to different cities three times. In the last years, Todd had begun to complain about everything that Christine did. She could do nothing the way he wanted it done.

Before coming to counseling, Todd had quit his current job

and accepted a position in another town. This time, Christine refused to move and wanted a divorce.

Todd was emotionally distraught and broken. He loved Christine more than anyone else in his life, and he realized that he had been "too hard" on her. Christine, having put up with the criticism and blame for so many years, had finally had enough. By the time they came to counseling, there was nothing left in the marriage for Christine. Shortly thereafter, they divorced.

Todd was a classic case of chronic discontent. Nothing ever seemed to please him, and he found a way to blame all of his frustration on the people around him. Slowly, all but his closest friends and family had distanced themselves from him, and eventually even his marriage collapsed as a result of his emotional blame.

It is difficult being in a relationship with someone with chronic discontent. When they are emotionally withdrawn *and* blaming you for all their frustrations, it becomes too much. Eventually it kills whatever love you have for the person. The one of the most tragic and costly games of all those played by CDers.

The Debtor Game

The debtor game is a subtle game that CDers played to control their tendency to withdraw. By driving themselves deep into debt, they quite literally put themselves into a financial straightjacket that prevents them from withdrawing from the established moorings of their lives. When you are laboring under a mountain of debt, you can't afford to change jobs, buy a new house or car, or get divorced. The chains of debt keep you strapped to the life that you've created.

The debtor game is a kind of "self-medication" used by some with chronic discontent to control their withdrawal symptoms. It doesn't make you feel better, but it does prevent you from running away.

The Wooden Leg Game

The game of wooden leg is played by blaming all your frustrations on a disability (e.g., "wooden leg") or unfortunate event in your life. The wooden leg can be anything from an abusive childhood to a failed business. "If it weren't for the bankruptcy, I'd be living the high life now."

Diane had a difficult childhood. Her father worked for an oil company and was working overseas for most of her younger years. Her mother drank heavily, and when Diane was 12, her mother died of alcoholism. After her mother's death, her father sent her away to boarding school.

As an adult, Diane had two failed marriages and was always on the verge of a bankruptcy. She had tried numerous careers and somehow was always able to squeeze out a living, but she never had much to spare.

Over the years, Diane had entered psychotherapy several times. Each time she would recount her miserable childhood and grieve over the effect it had had on her life. Whenever the therapist would nudge her to begin moving past her childhood and creating a life for herself, she would abruptly terminate therapy.

Now in her late forties, Diane still blames most of her problems on her childhood. What is clear is that Diane doesn't want to heal her childhood, *she wants to blame it*. Diane is using her wooden leg to exempt herself from responsibility for her life.

The truth is that everyone experiences some kind of debilitating event in life: painful childhood, a tragic accident, the death of child, or a messy divorce. As hurtful as these things can be, they give us a choice. We can either move through the pain and pick up the pieces of our lives, or we can give up in defeat. As difficult as it can be to move on with life, we must if we are to go on and experience any more of the joys life offers. Tragedy is always with us, and we never forget it.

Remembering tragedy and using it as an excuse for living are two very different things. When we play the game of wooden leg, we use the tragedy to escape our lives and as a reason for our chronic discontent.

The Blemish Game

The blemish game is played by focusing on some real or imagined flaw in a person when the relationship starts to become emotionally intimate. You focus on the way he eats and it repulses you. Or, you can't stop thinking about how loudly she talks and you stop spending time with her.

By obsessing on a negative trait, we actually convince ourselves that we don't like the person. We keep playing the game, time and again, moving through friends and lovers, none of whom met our standards.

What are we looking for in a friend? A lover? We can't say, but we can definitely tell you some of the things we don't want. That's because we spend far more time obsessing over faults than we do feeling good about another person. It's almost as if the first thing we do when we meet someone is to try and discover the critical flaw.

The game of blemish ultimately leaves us alone and isolated. Why? Because no one will ever be flawless in our eyes. Even if they are close to "perfection" we'll turn that into a flaw!

I'm reminded of a friend of mine in college whose mother never approved of his girlfriends. No matter who he brought home (and he brought home several), she found something wrong with them. Finally, when he brought home Andrea, his mother could find nothing immediately wrong with her, so behind her back she called Andrea "Little Miss Perfect." In an odd way, she flipped Andrea's good qualities into a negative so she could have her blemish.

The "Don't Tell Me What I'm Feeling" Game

The "don't tell me what I'm feeling" game is played by denying our feelings when someone else points them out.

- "Why are you angry with me?" Response: "I'm not angry."
- "You've been sulking all day." Response: "I'm perfectly happy."
- "You seemed to be excited about the job offer." Response: "It's just a job."

Having another person point out our feelings can be very threatening to someone with chronic discontent. We often work hard at hiding our feelings, and the last thing we want is someone else discovering them.

The key to understanding this game is the threat involved. Having someone else identify our feelings is very disconcerting for us. In response, we either deny the feeling or deliberately suggest that we are feeling something completely different, just to throw the other person off track.

Anger and protest is a common response by a CDer when confronted about a feeling. It seems intrusive and scary to have someone getting that close to our feelings and it elicits a reflex to push them away. Inevitably we say with our actions, "Don't tell me what I'm feeling!"

The Sexual Game

The sexual game is played by substituting sexual activity for emotional honesty. Sex feels intimate, but isn't necessarily. Whenever a relationship begins to become emotionally intimate, we switch into a sexual mode. The sexual game doesn't necessarily require that we have sex with the other person, only that we sexualize the situation.

Ron plays relies heavily on the sexual game to avoid emotional honesty. He has been married to Katina for five years, and his response to anything emotional, whether it is an argument or a celebration, is to seduce Katina into the bedroom. In Ron's mind, sex makes everything OK again.

When Ron is with his buddies after work, he often sexualizes those relationships, too. Whenever one of his buddies mentions a problem with his wife, Ron is ready with an off-color joke to "lighten things up." There's always a big laugh and the conversation turns toward something less serious. By talking and joking about sexual matters, Ron feels closer to his buddies without having to enter any emotional depth.

Historically, men have been the biggest players of the sexual game, but often women sometimes use it, too. For example, when a woman wants to feel more intimate with a man who doesn't open up emotionally, she may try to use sex as a way to open the door to a greater intimacy.

Some men and women who are extraordinarily attractive discover the sexual game early in life. They learn that they can manipulate others by acting sexual. Because others often respond very positively, they never learn the skills of emotional honesty.

8

The Legends of Discontent

(Do You Believe?)

Living with chronic discontent changes you. In fact, it changes everything about you. Slowly and subtly, like a vine that grows up the trunk of an old tree, chronic discontent wraps around every aspect of your life. The emotional shame, withdrawal and comeback affect all your relationships, your career, and even your leisure times. Eventually everything is touched by the consequences of emotional constriction.

An interesting thing happens when your life is swallowed by discontent: you start to see the world differently. You develop certain beliefs about life that support your experience of discontent, and then you project that experience onto other people. In other words, you begin to believe that the whole world is struggling with discontent, and you see them through that lens.

As a result, most people with chronic discontent hold a similar set of beliefs about how life works. It isn't that we necessarily get together and teach one another these beliefs, but rather they spring naturally from our lives after we struggle with discontent.

These beliefs play a prominent role in the "chronic" part of chronic discontent. First, they help you to make sense of your own suffering. Nobody wants to believe that they are suffering alone, and by adopting these beliefs, you convince yourself that your experience is not unique and that everyone around you is having the same experience. This is the process of validating your life—confirming to you that you are not alone in your experience. Validation is something everyone needs, not just people with chronic discontent.

Secondly, these beliefs serve the function of maintaining chronic discontent. In other words, as long as you hold these beliefs, you remain locked into the behavior patterns of chronic discontent.

Beliefs are nothing more than assumptions that we take for fact. You and I have many thousands of beliefs about our world and how it works, and these beliefs allow us to navigate through life more easily. For example, you might believe that your spouse loves you, and as a result, you don't have to constantly test the relationship to see if it is still strong when you are making daily decisions. Believing that your spouse loves you helps you live your life more efficiently unless, of course, that belief is false. As long as our beliefs are anchored firmly in reality, they are very helpful to us.

In this chapter we take a close look at the particular beliefs that develop and support chronic discontent. You might think of this chapter as the "creed of chronic discontent." In many ways it's like a statement of the church of chronic discontent that you unwittingly joined many years ago. You probably don't subscribe to every belief in this chapter, but chances are that you hold many, if not most of them, to be true.

Here's a quiz that will show you which of the beliefs you hold.

Chronic Discontent Beliefs Quiz

Remember, be honest and don't spend too much time on any one item. Give the first answer that comes to mind.

	YES	NO
1. I believe there is almost always a self-serving, hidden reason for other people's actions. I always look for this and do my best to uncover it.		
2. I believe that if I allow other people to see my vulnerable side, they will inevitably use it against me. I must never let my guard down.		
3. I believe that everyday life is basically boring and uninspiring. It is a mistake for me to expect more from life.		
4. I believe that fools are fools because they let their feelings interfere with their judgment. I must never make a decision upon my feelings.		
5. I believe that one day "my ship will come in" and I'll really be happy. I try to keep focused on that day.		
6. I believe that joy comes from escaping the straitjacket of everyday life. I escape as often as possible.		
7. I believe that friendships are often more work than they are worth. I only keep a few friends.		
8. I believe that if I don't get emotionally involved, I can't get hurt. I don't get emotionally involved.		
9. I believe that other people don't want to hear my problems. I keep my problems to myself.		
10. I believe it is best to keep my expectations low, then I can't be disappointed with the results. I focus on the worst-case scenario.		

	YES	NO
11. I believe that my life will feel better if I own more stuff. I buy happiness whenever I can.		
12. I believe that satisfaction in life comes from controlling my life as much as possible. I try to control everything that affects me.		
13. I believe that persistently cheerful people are superficial, dull, and probably not very smart. I avoid cheerful people.		

The items that you answered "yes" are chronic discontent beliefs that you hold. As you through this chapter, you pay close attention to these beliefs.

I Believe There Is Almost Always a Self-Serving, Hidden Reason for Other People's Actions. I Always Look for This and Do My Best to Uncover It.

After living through so many disappointments, we start to expect it everywhere and from everyone. It's a subtle cynicism that creeps into our lives and ultimately taints the expectations we have of other people. We become convinced that eventually everyone will disappoint, or maybe even hurt us.

Rather than waiting around for the other person to reveal how they will disappoint us, we strike a defensive and posture, and try to discover it beforehand. We aren't malicious or angry; usually, we are quite matter-of-fact about it.

This posture toward other people has a strong constricting effect on our relationships. It's difficult for us to make many new friends or to establish trusting business relationships. We come across to others as standoffish and not always an easy person to get to know.

Sometimes, our tendency to expect the worst in others causes us to withdraw from relationships that otherwise might be very helpful. An acquaintance of mine worked for a while as a literary agent who worked to acquire book contracts for aspiring authors. She worked hard at it and had a great eye for good writing. In fact, a few of her authors went on to have very successful careers.

My friend's chronic discontent ultimately undermined her relationships with the editors with whom she worked. With every new book deal that she brought to an editor, she expected the worst. When an editor didn't call back right away she would get defensive and angry, assuming that the editor didn't think highly enough of her to call back in a timely manner. Often, there were good reasons why the editor didn't call back. Maybe he was on vacation or was waiting to hear what his colleagues thought of the manuscript. Maybe, even he was trying to get approval from his superiors for more money to purchase the manuscript.

Assuming the worst in these cases, my friend would leave angry voicemails for the editor or maybe even go ahead and sell the manuscript to another publishing house without notifying the first editor with whom she was angry. The net effect was that she quickly gained a bad reputation in the literary business and found it increasingly difficult to sell her manuscripts to editors. Eventually, she was forced to make a career change and began a new career as a publicist for a magazine.

Like it was for my friend, holding the belief that "there is almost always a self-serving, hidden reason for other people's actions" causes us to withdraw from important relationships. Whether they are romantic, friendship, or business relationships, we withdraw because we assume the worst is true of other people. Rather than deal with the threatening feelings of rejection, we strike back by being the first to rejection the other person.

When we assume the worst in other people, we feel things like:

- My husband wants to go to marriage counseling so he can let me down easily and ease his conscious of any guilt for leaving me. (Instead of feeling that he might want to make the marriage better.)
- My boss gave me a raise because I've been there so long and my number was up. (Instead of feeling good about having been rewarded for a good job.)
- My friends say they like my paintings, but what else could they say? They're certainly not going to tell me to my face that I don't have any talent. (Instead of enjoying the compliments of close friends.)

I Believe That If I Allow Other People to See My Vulnerable Side, They Will Inevitably Use It Against Me. I Must Never Let My Guard Down.

Janice couldn't say, "I'm sorry." The words just wouldn't come out of her mouth no matter how sorry she really felt.

Her marriage to John had been a good one for the first six years, but after that things went wrong. By the time they celebrated their tenth anniversary, Janice and John were seeking marriage counseling for a marriage they both feared might be over.

In counseling, John talked about Janice in loving terms, but said that she had grown colder over the years. She never let her guard down, he said. She never let anyone inside where she really lived. He wished for once that she would acknowledge that she was human, like everyone else.

Whenever John would say something that had even the slightest tone of criticism to Janice, she would become angry and defensive. She'd start attacking him verbally, saying things like, "You think you're perfect" and "I'm tired of you always criticizing me." John felt like Janice had become so defensive in recent years that they couldn't talk about anything that was meaningful for fear that Janice might take some comment the wrong way and storm out of the room.

Janice sat through most of the counseling without saying much. Occasionally, she would burst into tears and tell John that she didn't want him to leave her, but that was all she could say. She never directly addressed his concerns, even when confronted by the counselor. She would quickly change the subject or simply stare at the floor.

Janice truly didn't want her marriage to end. She loved John. The truth that she couldn't express was that she lived under an enormous cloud of guilt about the marriage. Inside, she felt totally responsible for their problems and privately punished herself for not being a better wife. Unfortunately, she kept all of it inside and was never able to tell it to John.

Because Janice already felt terribly guilty over the marriage problems, whenever John said anything that suggested Janice was wrong or hurtful, it was too much for her to bear and she would attack back. Her overworked sense of responsibility had punished her severely and then having John add to that punishment was too painful.

Janice is like many people with chronic discontent. She grew up in an environment where any weakness was either punished or ridiculed mercilessly. With two older brothers who were fiercely competitive, she learned to never give anyone an opportunity to touch her vulnerabilities. As an adult, she continued this pattern long after having left her parents' home. It was deeply engrained in her that feelings were a sign of weakness and only invited attacks from others.

Now, her inability to show her vulnerable side was killing her marriage. If only John could see that side of her—the side she nourishes and protects from the rest of the world. If only he knew how responsible she felt and how sorry she truly was for her part in the failed marriage, he would feel differently about her and maybe want to stay and work things out.

Janice had no idea of how to start. The idea of spilling her inner feelings to John terrified her and momentarily made her think that it would be better to lose the marriage than to face the humiliation of showing her vulnerable side. She truly didn't want to lose John, but she was terrified and unable to give John what he wanted. To make matters worse, she feared that it was now too late, anyway. She had begun to feel that John had already decided to leave.

The truth is that when most people experience our vulnerabilities, it makes them feel more compassionate toward us. Because so many people with chronic discontent grew up in family circumstances where we were hurt or punished for being vulnerable, we assume that the rest of the world will do the same to us if given the opportunity. So we present a strong, sometimes unfeeling personality to the world and only privately nurse our more vulnerable side.

Hiding your vulnerable side might cause you to:

- Privately feel tender, caring feelings toward another, but never express those in a card or with flowers.
- Overly state your accomplishments and strengths as a way of covering up your insecurities and failings.
- Alienate others who are feeling vulnerable but don't sense that you can empathize with their feelings.

I Believe That Everyday Life Is Basically Boring and Uninspiring. It Is a Mistake for Me to Expect More from Life.

For most people suffering from chronic discontent, life is a bit of a chore that is on rare occasions punctuated with moments of excitement. We approach the day expecting it to be mundane and uninspiring.

Because we believe that life is more duty than inspiration, we live with a weight of lethargy on our backs, slowly bending us over and draining our energy.

For many years, I worked with corporate executives who were struggling with issues of life and career. One of the most remarkable things I learned from those experiences was that really successful executives had a passion for their work, and they often worked around the clock, seven days a week. You might expect that such a schedule would exhaust them and eventually burn them out, but it didn't. In fact, the passionate executives were energized by their work.

Since then, I've noticed that this held true for all people. When we love life, we're energized by it. When life is a chore, it drains us.

Sandra loves children. Her own children are grown and living on their own. Now in her fifties, Sandra owns a day-care center where she keeps 25 preschool children for up to twelve hours each day. You might think that she would be absolutely exhausted at the end of the day, but it just isn't so. Sandra is just as attentive to the crying boy with scraped knee at the end of the day as she is to the four-year-old girl who wants to talk about how her dog ate her doll first thing in the morning.

How does Sandra do it? She is excited about her work and sees wonderful possibilities in the children she keeps. She truly feels that she is doing something important in the world and expects that her life and the lives of the children are improved by what she does.

Those of us with chronic discontent have difficulty maintaining the enthusiasm and inspiration Sandra has for very long. We certainly *want* to have that kind of enthusiasm, but it just isn't there for us. We start out excited, but we know from experience that it will eventually wane, and what was once inspiration will morph into drudgery.

Because of our experiences, we cling to the belief that life is mostly dull and void of inspiration. As our chronic discontent grows, we no longer allow ourselves to get excited about a new project, home, relationship etc., because we know that the greater our excitement is at the outside, the more disappointed we will be when it wanes. In essence we believe, "If you don't expect much, you can't be disappointed with what you get."

So as a protective measure, we "ratchet down" what little excitement in life that we feel. We tell ourselves that it really isn't that great . . . there are probably problems we just haven't discovered . . . nothing is ever as good as it seems. In short, we sabotage our own excitement.

I Believe That Fools Are Fools Because They Let Their Feelings Interfere with Their Judgment. I Must Never Make a Decision upon My Feelings.

Let's face it, we just don't trust feelings, especially when it comes down to important life decisions.

Adrienne worked for a national retail company as buyer for women's clothing. She was also involved in the best relationship she had ever known. While she and Tony had discussed marriage, Adrienne's work schedule was so busy, there just hadn't been time to plan for a wedding.

Then, one day, the bomb dropped. Her company was relocating to Atlanta. Of course, she was guaranteed a job, but she would have to move to Atlanta if she wanted it.

The decision she faced was grueling. Would she look for another job and stay in New York (she was fairly confident that she could land another position quickly) or continue with her company, leave Tony, and move to Atlanta?

Financially the best decision was to move, since she had a few more years before being vested in the retirement plan. If she left now, she'd lose everything she had contributed to the plan. What her heart wanted most was to stay and make a life with Tony. It was a wrenching decision.

Adrienne moved to Atlanta, despite her feelings. She convinced herself that it just wasn't "smart" to not move, and she hoped that somehow she and Tony would work things out.

As it turned out, six months of a long-distance relationship strained their relationship and they grew farther apart. Eventually, they parted ways.

Coupled with the failure of the relationship, Adrienne was miserable in Atlanta. She hated the heat and humidity of the summer there and desperately missed the urban pleasures of New York. Every chance she got, she left Atlanta for New York.

Adrienne's decision to move to Atlanta is one that many of us with chronic discontent might make also. We discount the importance of our feelings, and instead make our decision based on what we think is "right" rather than what we desire. This kind of decision-making leads us to do things like:

- Take a job we that we hate because it is the best job for our career.

- Stay in a relationship that is abusive because it is financially the best thing to do.
- Live in an area that we dislike because the houses are cheaper there.

I Believe That One Day "My Ship Will Come In" and I'll Really Be Happy. I Try to Keep Focused On That Day.

Feelings don't exist in the future, so it's a safe place for those of us who are afraid of how we feel. Feelings only live in the present and are remembered about the past. The future hasn't happened, and so we have no feelings for it yet.

Think about this for a moment. When you think about what will happen next week or year, what do you feel? You might *think* that you will feel happy or sad about something that could happen, but you don't *feel* it until it happens.

Escaping to the future is a favorite pastime of people with chronic discontent. We think, "Won't it be great when the kids are out of college and we can travel?" Or, "When I finally lose these twenty pounds, then I will feel great about myself." Many of us do it all the time; we sacrifice today for the fantasy of the future. Emotionally, it's always safer to live in the future.

One of the ways we manage chronic discontent is by deliberately making the present less than it otherwise could be. In other words, even though we can afford to buy a house, we decide to remain in our cramped apartment. Or, we go back to college for another degree even though it really isn't necessary. As long as we are working toward some future goal, we can alleviate some of the dissatisfaction we feel in the present.

What's important to recognize is that *we can't allow our-*

selves to obtain our dream. Deep in our unconscious we know that if we attain the dream, it will only disappoint us. So we keep ourselves in a continual state of working toward something, but never achieving it. By doing everything just short of achieving the dream, we can imagine that there is something better for us in the future. As long as we don't attain our dream, we are never disappointed.

Living in the future and denying the present can cause us to:

- Be perpetual students, always imagining that the next degree will make our life better.
- To never get married because we are waiting for that perfect person. Since the perfect mate doesn't exist, we are never disappointed by marriage.
- To work in a job that we truly dislike simply because it pays well and will allow us to retire early. When the time comes for early retirement, we find a string of reasons why it isn't a convenient time to retire. As a result, we are never disappointed by retirement.

I Believe That Joy Comes from Escaping the Straitjacket of Everyday Life. I Escape As Often As Possible.

When you suffer with chronic discontent, one way to make yourself feel better is to escape your life for a while. Escaping may not make you happy, but it does bring relief from the frustration of your life. Consider how some people with chronic discontent escape:

- Jon was lucky that he had a job that paid him very handsomely. He didn't much care for the work, but he loved the paycheck. Virtually every weekend and holiday he would escape to some exotic location. Whether it was Miami Beach or Costa Rica, he thought nothing of hopping on a plane with little more than his toothbrush. For Jon, happiness in life was all about escape.

- Betty managed her chronic discontent by scheduling an escape every day of the week. One day she would get a massage. The next day, she would spend a couple of hours with a trainer at the gym. The next day, it was a manicure. Even if it was just for an hour, she was able to forget about herself and her life. Escaping made life bearable.

- Rita was a shopper. She liked to call shopping her "walking meditation." She once said, "When I get behind a shopping cart, there's something that happens and the rest of life just melts away." It didn't matter whether it was clothes or kitchen gadgets, shopping was her escape, and she did it as often as possible.

- Don loved to drink beer. Every night after work, he would sit on the couch and drink a six-pack. It didn't matter what was on the television, he would park himself in front of it and drink the night away. He didn't think he was alcoholic; after all, he held a good job and didn't beat his wife. No, he was convinced that evenings were "his time" and as long as he kept paying the bills, he could drink as much beer as he pleased.

There are many ways of escaping your life—probably as many ways as there are people. And there's nothing wrong with escape. In moderation, it can be quite a necessary and healthy part of your life.

Escape is a problem is a serious problem when we must use it in order to feel something positive. To say that it brings CDers joy is a misnomer—all it really brings us is relief.

Relief from the continual disappointment and frustration.

Relief from the constant boredom.

Relief from the emotional void in our lives.

This kind of escape used as an emotional kick start, is dangerous and ultimately dysfunctional. It is especially dangerous, when we become over-reliant and addicted to it, as in the examples above. Too much escape begins to destroy the fabric of our lives. As with Don, it can even threaten our health, and ultimately our lives.

To help you recognize the difference between healthy and unhealthy escape, think of it this way:

- Healthy escape provides you with a pleasant change of scenery or consciousness.
- Unhealthy escape is a required for you to feel better.

The reason so many sufferers of chronic discontent fall into trouble with escape is because it is the only way they can feel some relief, even if for a brief while. We become dependent upon it to feel something good. For example, we can't enjoy a party without having a cocktail or two. Or, we don't have an enjoyable weekend unless we buy something for ourselves. Whatever the favorite escape might be, we rely on it as way of filling the emotional void and elevating our mood.

I Believe That Friendships Are Often More Work Than They Are Worth. I Only Keep a Few Friends.

Close friendships are difficult for people with chronic discontent. It's not that we aren't friendly—we are. And it's not that we don't like the idea of having friends—we do. The problem for us lies in the realities of friendship. The truth is, we often "use" friends. Let me explain with an example:

Camille is married and has three young children. Ever since her days in the college sorority, she has stayed in touch with the group women she knew there. Even though it had been fifteen years since college, they were still her closest friends.

Her pattern with her group friends was to have a short period of close communication followed by long periods of minimal contact. Whenever something would happen in her life when she needed the support of her friends, she'd call them up and it felt like old times again. Whether it was the birth of her children, the death of her mother, or when she left her career to be a stay-at-home mom, she would reconnect with her friends and they'd help her through it.

In recent years, however, she noticed that her friendships didn't seem very close. On the occasions that she would call, they were distant and less warm. Had she done something to offend them?

What Camille didn't realize was that she wasn't a very good friend. She wasn't "there" for her friends and usually only called when she needed them. She didn't have the skills or patience for an ongoing, close connection with her friends, so she'd pop in and out of their lives at times when she was feeling vulnerable and lonely.

It is amazingly common how many of us with chronic discontent treat our friends just as Camille did. We don't realize that we are "using" them, and we certainly don't mean to be hurtful. The honest truth is that we aren't capable of maintaining an ongoing, emotional relationship. The reality of such a friendship scares us away.

As a result, our friends tend to be more surface relationships, like the people we work with or our neighbors. We are friendly and talkative when we encounter them, but once they (or we) move on to another job or neighborhood, we typically move on to other surface relationships.

Take a minute and think on this. Are you consistently there for the person you consider your closest friend, or do you reconnect mostly when you are feeling lonely or vulnerable? Are the people who are in your immediate social group people who really know you and what you feel, or are they more acquaintances and/or business relations? If so, you've got to face the hard truth that you usually make an effort to be friendly when you need a friend, but don't follow through carefully with the friendship at other times. It isn't something that we want to believe is true about ourselves, but too often it is.

I Believe That If I Don't Get Emotionally Involved, I Can't Get Hurt. I Don't Get Emotionally Involved.

John doesn't get involved in his employees' lives. Unless someone else does it, he doesn't acknowledge birthdays, anniversaries, or other "personal" milestones. He doesn't socialize with the employees or customers after work hours. He doesn't keep pictures of his children on his desk, and privately he thinks it's a bad idea for people to drag their personal items into work. It's cleaner if you keep work—well, just work.

John works long hours during the weekdays. He struggled hard to build his grocery supply business, and even though it has grown, it never seems to reach a place where he feels secure in letting other people run the business. He prefers to be involved in most everything that happens around the company.

A few years back, he had an employee that had been with him for many years lose a daughter in a drunk-driving accident. It was a devastating loss to the employee. John sent flowers to the funeral, and later sent word to the employee to take a few weeks off with pay, but other than that, he never spoke with the employee about the tragedy.

At work, everyone respects John but no one feels particularly close to him. All they know of him is what they see at work—the hardworking boss. That's why they were all shocked when one of them saw buried in the legal notices of the local paper that John had recently filed for divorce from his wife of more than 20 years. He never once mentioned it at work, and no felt comfortable asking him about it.

Privately John had entered therapy because he was feeling depressed. The divorce had been long and drawn out and he didn't feel like his life was really worth much. Sure, he'd built a successful business, but it didn't mean all that much to him.

Although John had lived, worked, and raised two children in the same community, he couldn't name one person that he felt comfortable calling and just "shooting the breeze." There wasn't really anyone with whom he felt that comfortable.

For most of his life, John had practiced the belief that it's better not to get emotionally involved. "If you get involved in other people's business, it only serves you right when you get hurt." In his mind, every close relationship eventually ended in hurt.

Many people with chronic discontent are like John; we stand on the sidelines of life, looking over the field and players, but never allowing ourselves to become a player "because they might get hurt." We are observers of life, not participants.

This affords people with chronic discontent the unique opportunity to live with certain smugness toward others. We are beholden to no one. In many ways, we live above the emotional soup that engulfs the lives of those around us. In the good times, we think of ourselves as slightly superior. In the bad times, we feel terribly empty, and maybe even despondent.

But there comes a day—and it always comes—when we desperately need to feel our lives. We want what others have—the close, caring relationships. The weekends away with good friends. Romance with a special person. We crave these things and find our aloofness toward the untidiness of intimacy has led us down a lonely and ultimately disappointing path.

I Believe That Other People Don't Want to Hear My Problems. I Keep My Problems to Myself.

People with chronic discontent can be very good about putting on a game face for other people. No matter what turmoil is swirling in our lives, we can be skilled at hiding it from those around us. Telling other people our problems can create an emotionally charged situation that we'd rather avoid. We feel safer keeping it to ourselves.

The night that Jim, Donna's son, was arrested, was a shocking experience for Donna's parents. They had no idea that Jim had been in so much trouble in recent years and how difficult it had been for Donna and her husband. They had tried everything they knew to do, but still Jim would wind up skipping school or smoking pot behind the convenience store or, what finally landed him in jail, shoplifting. As parents, they were at the end of their rope.

For the past five years, since Jim was eight years old, he had been constantly in trouble at school and at home. Donna, who spoke to her mother by phone several times a week and visited her parents every few months, never mentioned anything about it. Her parents had noticed that Jim seemed to be a bit of a handful when he visited them, but they had assumed it was just because he was away from home. Donna had kept it all to herself. Even her closest friends had only been told part of the story.

Donna called that night to ask her father what to do. He had an attorney for many years and she needed advice on how to handle the situation. Over the phone she had to quickly tell the story of the numerous truancy arrests, etc. and why Jim was now in serious trouble. Donna's parents hung up the phone stunned and deeply saddened that their daughter had kept something so tragic from them.

Like Donna's parents, we often hurt those closest to us by not fully disclosing the details of our lives to them. Without thinking, we simply edit what we tell, removing all the emotional components. When they discover that we haven't been completely revealing and honest, it makes them feel as if we don't trust them with the important parts of our lives.

Of course, that's not why we don't share our problems. It makes us feel vulnerable, even around those we trust the most, so we keep them to ourselves. We'd rather suffer privately than to have those difficult conversations.

What sometimes happens to us is that the problem situations in our lives continue to grow until they burst onto the scene and suddenly everyone is aware of them. Like the situation with Jim's arrest, suddenly Donna's problem with her son is a very public matter.

Keeping our problems to ourselves causes significant stress on our relationships. Examples of how this happens include:

- Joe didn't tell his wife about having invested a significant portion of their retirement savings into a technology stock. When the stock unexpectedly took a nosedive, he held on hoping it would eventually come back and make up the losses. Now the stock is almost worthless and their savings have been dramatically diminished. One afternoon, his wife happened to open the brokerage statement . . .
- Karen didn't want to tell her family about the lump the doctor found in her breast. After all, the doctor was confident that radiation would completely remove the tumor. Now, six months later, the cancer has grown and the doctor has recommended that Karen have a radical surgical procedure. Her family is deeply hurt when they discover that she went through so much of this trauma alone.
- Joan was embarrassed that her husband sometimes drank too much. When he'd get drunk, he would often become angry, and on a few occasions, he hit her. Tonight, she found herself pulling into the driveway of her closest friend with a broken arm and black eye after one of his rampages. Her friend, who had no idea this had been going on, was stunned and deeply saddened that Joan hadn't asked for help until now.

Trusting relationships are based as much on sharing our problems as our achievements with others. When we withhold any part of ourselves, those around us feel betrayed and hurt. Why have we not trusted them? Do we care so little for them that we didn't bother to tell them?

I Believe It Is Best to Keep My Expectations Low, Then I Can't Be Disappointed with the Results. I Focus On the Worst-Case Scenario.

I have to admit that this belief was one of my favorites. I prided myself in always considering the worst-case scenario whenever I made a decision. Could I live the absolute worst?

Why did I (and other CDers) do this? Mostly because we can't handle the added disappointment of having our expectations not met. If we only expect the worst, then we're never disappointed. It protects us from those unwelcome feelings.

The problem with this belief is that we soon come to expect the worst in everything, and slowly our outlook on life becomes rather dim. The job will probably take us nowhere and be full of frustrations. The marriage will probably end in divorce. Our children will probably become less than they are capable of becoming.

How this sometimes manifests is when something goes wrong, we immediately assume the worst.

- Your husband doesn't come home for dinner, so you imagine he's having an affair.
- You weren't invited to an acquaintance's wedding, so you assume that the oversight was intentional and the person doesn't care for you.
- The car repair bill was significantly higher than you expected, so you imagine that the mechanic thinks you're naïve and is ripping you off.

Of course, these kinds of over-reactions create all kinds of difficulties for us in relationships. More often than not, the ill intent we have imagined isn't true, but we've reacted as if it is. In the end, we destroy relationships that could have been very good for us simply because we always expected the worst from the other person.

The shame and regret that floods us after having over-reacted is very painful. More than once I heard myself saying "I did it again" after discovering that I had been gruff with someone for an imagined reason that turned out not to be true. I'd feel horrible and start to think that there was something really wrong with me that I couldn't step back from these situations and find out the facts before reacting. I had come to expect the worst-case so strongly, that I often just assumed that was what had happened before I knew the facts.

I Believe That My Life Will Feel Better if I Own More Stuff. I Buy Happiness Whenever I Can.

Money is the consolation prize most Americans have chosen to give themselves, in lieu of a rich, fulfilling life. It is so much a part of our culture, advertisement-driven entertainment, and social life that many of us never realize the extent to which we use money to deaden the ache of our inner emptiness. We've convinced ourselves that we'd feel differently if we only had a bigger house, a better car, a higher salary, or could retire earlier.

The tragedy of all consolation prizes is that they never really replace what we really want. Money doesn't make us feel one bit better. Let me tell you a true story:

Ken and Sylvia dated in college and were married the year after they both graduated in the mid-1960s. Both quickly found themselves in good jobs in New York City, with increasing responsibility. They worked hard, determined to never have to live as their blue-collar parents had lived. For the first ten years of their marriage they lived in a very small one bedroom apartment in a not-so-well-to-do section of Brooklyn. They saved every dime they could by never taking vacations and living quite frugally. In time, they saved enough to buy a place of their own, also a small one-bedroom flat, but this time in Manhattan, closer to their offices.

Both chronic discontent sufferers, their marriage was less than fulfilling for both of them. They often quarreled and spent most evenings sitting quietly in front of the television or separately at the gym or tennis court. Their lives had acquired a very predictable pace that was deadening in its boredom but also secure and manageable.

In their late thirties, both Ken and Sylvia decided that having children might help enrich their lives, so they began saving again, this time for a larger place that could accommodate children. Within just a few years, they had enough money, moved and shortly thereafter were pregnant with their first child.

Six weeks after their son, Josh, was born, Sylvia returned to work after hiring a live-in nanny. The nanny was expensive, but took wonderful care of Josh. Life hummed along for a few more years until it was time to place Josh in a pre-school. They researched the finest pre-schools available and after much interviewing and letter-writing, acquired a space for Josh in one of the best pre-schools in Manhattan. As you can imagine, it was outrageously expensive, but Ken and Sylvia both thought that giving their child the very best would make them feel good.

In the meantime, their marriage had become more of a routine than a relationship. They shared very few common interests besides their son, and rarely, if ever, had the time or energy to pursue more romantic endeavors. There was a time when Sylvia thought that Ken might be having an affair with another woman, but Ken denied it and she never found any evidence to support her suspicions.

They gave Josh the best money could buy, including private schools, vacations in the Hampton's (so he would be around other educated boys from wealthy families), and eventually an undergraduate Ivy-League degree and a MBA. By the late-1980s, Josh had moved to the West Coast to take a position with a well-known high-tech firm.

With their only child gone, it was now just the two of them again. They had both done well in their careers and were making more money than ever. Finally, the time had come when they could live their dream.

Now, they ate out whenever they felt like it, took exotic vacations, and gave themselves whatever they wanted—including a wonderful second home in Boca Raton, Florida. On the surface, they finally made it. Underneath it all, they were miserable. When they were together on vacation or in Florida, they often bickered about small things like where to eat or when to take the boat out. The truth was, they were like strangers who lived with one another out of habit. Neither knew much about the inner life and feelings of the other. After having spent so much time together and covered so many miles, they were each separately determined to keep the marriage together, even though neither could say that they enjoyed spending time with the other.

The story of Ken and Sylvia is repeated a thousand times over every generation of CDers. We fool ourselves into believing that money and all the things it buys, like great educations, comfortable homes, and unusual vacations will make us fulfilled. We invest all the energy we have into making more money to acquire these things, all in hopes that they will make us happier.

But they never do. You'll be just as miserable in a one-room apartment as you will in the fanciest mansion on the hill. Money doesn't change anything, really. Once you move beyond the amount you need to survive—and that is really surprisingly little—it does very little to improve the experience of your life.

As I write these words, I know you must be thinking, "Well, I'm not so sure. I'd be happy if I had more money." If you're thinking that, I understand. Many of us with chronic discontent have believed this for all our lives. Just a little more will do. Just enough to buy house . . . buy a bigger house . . . join the country club . . . pay off our children's college . . . buy a vacation house on the beach. It goes on and on. If you haven't yet had the experience of making more money, then you'll have to take this on faith from the masses of people who have. Money doesn't make you happier.

A good friend of mine and I were laughing the other day as we hiked around the beaches at the foot of the Golden Gate bridge. My friend now owns a very successful furniture design business that is featured in all the best interior design magazines. We were laughing because he remembered an incident many years ago when I was working for a very large company and he was just a poor graduate student struggling to get by. He reminded that I had once told him quite seriously that it was difficult to get by on less than $150,000 a year (a very handsome salary for the time). Imagine that! I must admit, I remember saying it, too. The truth was, $150,000 didn't make me happy then. No matter how much I made, there was always something I couldn't buy or some trip I couldn't take. Somehow, I fooled myself into believing that it was lack of money that kept me from feeling fulfilled. I was truly imprisoned by the golden handcuffs of chronic discontent.

Take a good, long look at your life and ask yourself if you've been using money to fill the void of chronic discontent. Have you convinced yourself that shopping is the way to feel good about life? Have you been accumulating possessions and toys with the unspoken idea that if you get enough you will be happy? Have you told yourself that your misery is because you simply can't pay your bills? Are you trying to feel good about yourself by having lots of money?

I Believe That Satisfaction In Life Comes from Controlling My Life As Much As Possible. I Try to Control Everything That Affects Me.

Martha gave up her career to have children. Now she plans everything for them, never lets them out of her sight for even a second, and even does their school homework for them at times . . .

Dave is a supervisor at the local container plant. He hates his job, but has resigned himself to finishing out his career there. Everyone knows that he is the most difficult boss in the plant to work for. He insists that every job be done exactly the way he would do it . . .

Pat is a magazine editor for a neurological trade publication. She had always dreamed of working for a big fashion magazine with glossy photos of models wearing the latest style, but instead she's stuck with photographs of half-sectioned brains and scientific text that puts even some neurologists to sleep. The writers that work for her secretly call her the "dragon lady" for her irritable moods and compulsive need to rewrite every single sentence of her writers' articles prior to publication . . .

These are the stories of chronically discontent people who

try to console themselves by controlling other people. The truth is that they are caught in a personal crisis of disappointment and frustration about their own lives but feel that they can't do anything about it. So, they reach out to other people and try to control them.

The use of control as a consolation prize can be complex, but it is also very common. It usually starts with blame.

Those of us with chronic discontent are often masters at blaming others for our own disappointment and frustration. For example, it sounds something like this:

"If I wasn't married to such a jerk, then I'd be OK."

"If it weren't for this job, I'd be really happy."

"If it weren't for the kids, we wouldn't have these financial worries."

"If my friends were more supportive, then I could be successful."

Many people use this kind of "blame-scaping" as a method to avoid taking responsibility for their problems, but those with chronic discontent are often very practiced at it. And blame is nothing more than the beginning of control.

The unspoken logic goes something like this: "You are responsible for my problems, therefore I must change, manipulate, or guilt you into doing differently so that I can feel better."

Ralph tells me of a time, a few years back, when he was in college and discovered that the money his father had been setting aside for his tuition and expenses had never been given to him. The way Ralph's parent's managed their household expenses was that Ralph's father would give his mother a "paycheck" every month out of which all expenses were to be paid, including Ralph's living expenses at college. Ralph, unaware previously that this was the arrangement hadn't received any money and was working several jobs just to pay rent and buy food. When he found out the truth, he was furious and called his mother to ask why she hadn't forwarded the money to him while he was away at college. Rather than dealing with what had happened, his mother went to bed for days telling everyone that her son had been horrible to her. In a few days, Ralph's father called and demanded that he apologize for "whatever it was that he did to his mother." When Ralph told his father the story, his father told him to apologize to his mother anyway. From then on, Ralph's father sent a monthly check directly to him. As far as he knows, the issue about the money was dropped.

Ralph's mother is an excellent example of how we blame others for our feelings (or lack of) and then attempt to control other people into making us feel better. By going to bed for days and making everyone in the household miserable, she was able to manipulate them into catering to her and even coaxed an apology for something that was clearly her fault.

Maybe you and I don't use control as dramatically (or deviously) as Ralph's mother, but we often use it in an attempt to make ourselves feel something.

Chronic discontent makes us feel out of control of our own lives, because no matter what we try, we always seem to feel frustration and disappointment. We start to feel helpless about our own ability to change our lives for the better and get the things we want out of life. So what choices do we have? Many of us begin trying to control other people's lives, particularly those who are emotionally attached to us, like spouses and children. These people, we discover, can be manipulated into making us feel better for the moment. If we make them feel sorry enough for us, they bring us presents, cook us wonderful meals, or take us on vacations that make us feel better for a while. If we make them feel guilty, then they are less likely to confront us with our own shortcomings. If we make them feel responsible for our feelings, then we create "emotional slaves" who are always at our service, trying to make us feel better.

Like money, control is very common consolation prize among those with chronic discontent. It's tough to admit that you've been using it on those you love. I know—my own experience of acknowledging this was deeply painful. It's really important, however, that you come to terms with the way you've controlled other people in an attempt to quell your frustration over feeling out of control of your own life.

An extremely effective way of helping yourself to break this habit is to apologize to those you've attempted to control in the past. As part of your apology, give them permission to point out to you when attempt to control them again in the future. Trust me, you'll probably slip back into the old control habit again, and when you do, they'll be there to tell you about it. It isn't fun, but it's a powerful way of helping yourself to stop something that can eventually destroy your relationships with those you love. Think about how important this is, how much you love them, and I know you'll find the courage within yourself to apologize. If you really are serious about giving up this consolation prize, this will work for you.

I Believe That Persistently Cheerful People Are Superficial, Dull, and Probably Not Very Smart. I Avoid Cheerful People.

This belief is a favorite among academics, writers, scientists, and other intellectuals who suffer from chronic discontent. It probably won't surprise you to learn that it's also a favorite among some psychotherapists.

In short, when your life is flooded with disappointment and frustration, you try to feel better by telling yourself that any-one else who appears to be happy is probably lying, stupid, or both. You pat yourself on the back with a comforting "There, there. Everyone is as miserable as I am." The thought that someone else might be truly happy makes your own disap-pointment all the more intense.

The first time I remember seeing this belief for what it is was back in college. I had a brilliant statistics professor who held several Ph.D.s in psychology, statistics and mathematics. He was probably one of the most intelligent people I've ever met.

Psychology students aren't known for their love of math, especially not if their major is in clinical psychology. They prefer the more creative pursuits, and often have an uncanny fear of numbers.

This professor, I'll him Dr. Hicks, prided himself on humil-iating students, especially if they seemed the least bit cheerful. On more than a few occasions I watched him drill a student in front of the class to the point of utter humiliation and tears. Once he reached that point, he would let up and move on to the next topic.

Was Dr. Hicks a sadist who got his jollies from torturing and humiliating otherwise bright and capable students? I don't think so. He's like so many intellectuals, although his methods were much more extreme. He needed to feel that no one else was happier or more fulfilled than he was. It became his mis-sion in life to prove to others just how insignificant and error-prone they were. It made his own misery less painful when he could prove, if even for a moment, that other people were as miserable as he was.

Newly trained psychotherapists sometimes fall into this trap. When a client bounds in the door and says that she is having a great day, the therapist starts to probe into painful issues that the client might be repressing with this show of happiness. Of course, this might be the case, but it isn't always—not by a long shot. It's possible to happy, even giddy without being in denial of some painful feeling. But, of course, when those joyous feelings are strangers to the therapist, they appear as signs of the client's dysfunction.

In some areas of academic study and professional practice, it's considered a sign of low intellect to not be tormented with chronic discontent. After all, if you are really grasping the existential realities of this world, how can you possibly be happy?

9

Discontented Relationships

(Which Ones Do You Keep?)

Perhaps the most difficult problem for the chronically discontent is found in relationships. Relationships are the source of strong feelings; indeed, almost all feelings. Being involved with another person, whether in romance, business, friendship or family, presents the constant potential for emotional entanglement. People with chronic discontent aren't comfortable with their own feelings, much less dealing with the feelings of someone else. As a result, our relationships suffer.

There is tragic fact that exists in the relationships of those of us with chronic discontent: *We often choose to be in relationships with other people who are emotionally withdrawn.* It's just more comfortable to be with someone we know will never require us to expose our feelings or force us into an emotional corner.

Of course, the problem is here that you now have not just one, but two people with chronic discontent. Both are actively avoiding emotional self-disclosure, so the relationship stands virtually no chance of experiencing emotional flow. The result is a relationship that is a connection, but nothing more. It leaves us feeling safe, but unsatisfied.

The Relationships That Fail Us

You may recall from earlier chapters that emotional flow is what creates contentment. In relationships, CDers rarely, if ever, achieve flow, so they are left with relationships that never get past the connection stage.

In this chapter, we look at the kinds of dissatisfying relationships that sufferers from chronic discontent often find themselves in. I call them "connections" because that's all they are—a connection, most often between two people who have colluded together to hide their feelings.

Discontented Relationships Quiz

For the questions below, answer "yes" if it describes a relationship (friendship, romantic, or otherwise) that you are currently in or have been part of in recent memory.

	YES	NO
1. The relationship starts and moves very quickly. In no time, it occupies a good deal of your time and attention.		
2. The relationship ends abruptly with one person suddenly becoming unavailable.		
3. The relationship is filled with activity but not much emotional sharing.		
4. The relationship is based on common activities (working out, golf, playing bridge, etc.)		
5. The relationship is an attempt to be closer to someone who is more beautiful, rich, powerful, etc.		

	YES	NO
6. One or both people in the relationship use their physical attractiveness to manipulate the other.		
7. The relationship is that one person is always taking care of the other person.		
8. The relationship is between adults, but is similar to a parent-child relationship.		
9. The relationship is based on a common obsession or appetite (drinking buddies, etc.)		
10. All your relationships are centered upon a single activity or focus.		
11. The relationship is friendly and interesting, but lacks any real personal depth.		
12. The relationship is based on a common interest or goal, but never seems to go further.		

SCORING

The items that you answered "yes" are associated with one of discontented relationships you may keep. Look over the quiz and for any item that you answered "yes," find the associated relationship in the table below.

Items	Relationship
1–2	Immediate connection
3–4	Activity connection
5–6	Narcissistic connection
7–8	Unindividuated connection
9–10	Addiction connection
11–12	Intellectual connection

THE IMMEDIATE CONNECTION

Week One: "Honey, you are the most beautiful and sensual woman I've ever known. I find myself thinking about you all the time. All I want to do is to be with you."

There are touching cards, flowers, and candlelight dinners. The relationship is moving fast and sweeping you away. It's scary and thrilling.

Week Two: "Where have you been all my life? You're the one I've been looking for."

The relationship is the perfect romance. It's only a week old, but it seems like something you've been wanted for years, but could never find. What difference does time make when you've finally met The One!

Week Three: "It's you and me forever. We're meant to be together."

Now you've moved from romance to weddings and more. You start to plan your life in terms of "us" and "we." Your friends are happy for you, but a bit concerned that you've only known each other for a short period.

Week Four: Nothing. Calls aren't returned. You're left hanging.

Week Five: Still nothing.

Week Six: "Where is he?"

Week Seven: "I guess it must be over."

The immediate connection blows into your life, stands on the balcony professing eternal love, seems to share his deepest secrets with you, and then is suddenly gone. There are no harsh words. No reasons for the breakup. Just silence. You're left to assume that it is over.

It doesn't do you much good to confront the immediate connection at this point. He'll be superficially kind and give you plenty of evasive reasons. Too busy. Work is overwhelming.

His parents are in town. He's been sick. Still, he doesn't call. The next thing you hear is that he's been about town with someone else on his arm.

Is the immediate connection just a jerk who uses romance as an entrée to sex? Maybe. Is he a con man who truly cares little for his victims, but knows how to play the game to his advantage? Perhaps. There's also a good chance that he's chronically discontent. He craves intimacy and emotionally honesty, and this craving drives him to extremes. He comes on extra strong and gets a taste of what he needs, and then the shame kicks in and he runs scared. The immediate connection is caught between what he wants and what he fears, emotional honesty; so he vacillates between extreme intimacy and withdrawal.

Of course, the immediate connection can be male or female. In fact, the immediate connection may not be a lover at all. She can be a business associate who promises the moon and then vanishes or the friend who calls you every hour and then suddenly stops without explanation. Anyone who suffers with chronic discontent can get caught in the cycle of the immediate connection relationship. The strong magnetic pull of the craving for emotional honesty and a corresponding fear of the same pull you between two extremes.

What's the payback for creating immediate connection relationships? It is a temporary fulfillment of the need for emotional honesty without the long-term consequences of such a relationship. Those who depend on the immediate connection relationships for all their needs find themselves constantly preoccupied with creating and leaving intense relationships.

Think of it this way. It's easy to pour your heart out to an anonymous stranger that you know won't be part of your life forever. You unload your burden and get a taste of compassion and validation without the long-term obligation of maintaining the relationship. That's what the immediate connection does, time and again.

The cost of populating your life with immediate connection relationships is enormous. The energy and time required for such intense, short-lived encounters consumes much of your daily attention. In the meantime, you have little time left for the other parts of your life.

THE ACTIVITY CONNECTION

Suddenly you are swept away—literally. Tonight is yoga followed by a barbecue with friends. Tomorrow night is cocktails at a work-related reception and then dinner at the newest trendy eatery. This weekend is a quick visit to the "cabin" where the days are filled with visits to Home Depot and do-it-yourself construction projects and the evenings are spent hopping from cocktails to dinner with you-know-who. The world of the hyperactive relationship is always on the move and the faster, the better.

The common ground that is found in the activity connection is based on adrenaline and excitement. What happens is that the person who initiates the relationship pulls the other person into a whiz-bang world of swirling, nonstop activity. There is no need, time, or energy to make an emotional exchange in this relationship.

Think of the star athlete or cheerleader from high school who won truckloads of friends by virtue of their activities, not because they learned to be a true friend. Later in life, they repeat the same patterns by becoming the present of the Junior League or perhaps by becoming president of the country club. Rather than making an emotional connection with others, they share activities with them. A relationship to this person is a commitment to share activities—not feelings.

Whenever the relationship runs aground, their inevitable solution is to schedule another activity. What we need is to go on a cruise! That will make our relationship better.

Beth and Sage are friends. They golf together every Wednesday morning and play bridge on Friday afternoon. They go on vacations together with their husbands and often attend each other's children's musical recitals and sports events. Their friendship has been nonstop action.

Then one day Sage told Beth she was divorcing her husband. It was certainly a traumatic event for Sage, but Beth struggled with it, too. She realized that she didn't know much about her friend Sage's inner thoughts and feelings. The two of them had spent uncountable hours together, yet they were more like ships passing in the night than real friends. She thought that Sage and her husband were very happy together. She was completely taken back by Sage's news.

In another case, Brad told his parents that he was gay. His father, trying to be as supportive as possible, said "I don't think I know anyone else who is gay." Brad looked at him in told disbelief and then said, "What do you think Roger, your business partner, is? And what about Dan, the barber, you've been seeing every three weeks for twenty years?" The truth was that Brad's father had spent endless hours with each of these men, but had never really made an emotional connection. His father's relationships were mostly based on activities, like business deals and haircuts, and not emotional connections.

Many professional people with chronic discontent maintain activity connections. The other person often assumes that the person with chronic discontent is too busy or too important to take the time to get really personal with them, so they accept a relationship that is based on mutual activities. It's not unusual for someone with chronic discontent to sometimes spend decades in a relationship with a friend or business associate and know very little about his or her personal life.

THE NARCISSISTIC CONNECTION

Those people with chronic discontent who are physically attractive sometimes rely on their looks to create and maintain relationships. All their lives people have wanted to be near them because they were beautiful, so they never had to learn the skills of an emotionally engaged relationship. They are accustomed to people wanting to be near them. They have the illusion of emotional connection without having to give anything in return.

What exchanges do occur in a narcissistic connection are best described as admiration and adoration. The other person's purpose in the relationship is to remind the beautiful person how wonderful she is.

So what's the payback for participating in such a relationship? The other person in this relationship gets pride and accomplishment by association. They know other people are jealous of their relationship with the beautiful person, and in a twisted way, it boosts their self-esteem.

Certainly not all attractive people create narcissistic connections, but many with chronic discontent do. It is a lifelong habit that allows them to fill their life with admiring people without having to reciprocate with an emotional exchange.

If you make the mistake of asking the narcissistic connection for something from the heart, you only get more beauty in return. "What more do you want from me?" she might ask.

After all, she's lending the aura of her beauty to you, isn't that generous enough?

Narcissistic connections aren't just with beautiful people. They happen with people who are very successfully, wealthy, powerful or popular, too. When a person has something that she believes that another person wants, she can use that asset as the basis of a relationship instead of an emotional exchange.

I've often heard the story told around about an author who has written several books and decided that the only way she could become a really great author was to appear on *The Oprah Winfrey Show*. She did everything imaginable to get close to Oprah—things like joining the gym where it was rumored that Oprah exercised and by mailing copies of her book those who were close to Oprah.

To my knowledge, Oprah was never aware of the attempts of this author to gain access to her. Nor was she aware of how much this author spoke of her and how much time the author spent trying to contact her.

This author is the kind of person that falls prey to a narcissistic connection. While I can't imagine that Oprah would do it, many powerful people use these people as substitutes for their own lack of emotionally honest relationships. They decorate their lives with needy people who are just happy to be near them. These people will tell them whatever they want to hear and never challenge them when they are wrong. More than a few top corporate executives and world leaders have fallen in the trap of creating narcissistic connections with their subordinates, and the results have been disastrous. For example, it's been noted by historians that President Lyndon Johnson's decision to escalate the Vietnam War was a direct result of having surrounded himself with advisors who didn't confront him on difficult issues.

THE UNINDIVIDUATED CONNECTION

The unindividuated connection involves a "mama's boy" or a "daddy's girl." These are relationships involving adults who have never cut the apron strings with their parents and become his or her own individual ("individuated"). Instead, the primary source of his emotional life is his relationship with his parents. Even if the parents are absent or long since dead, the unindividuated connection continues just as soon as a surrogate parent can be found.

Let me give you an example of how an unindividuated connection works. Donny was his mama's boy. She doted on him and cared for his every need. Donny never had to deal with the consequences of his behavior because his mother was always there to clean up the mess.

As an adult, Donny married Rachel. From the beginning of Donny and Rachel's relationship, he expected Rachel to take the place of his mother who had died a few years earlier. He stayed out until the early hours of the morning and became furious if Rachel questioned his whereabouts. He did absolutely nothing around the house and expected Rachel to do all the housework, shopping, and cooking. Whenever Donny was frustrated, he somehow expected Rachel to be there comforting him the way his mother had comforted him. If she didn't, he would fly into a rage and storm out of the house.

Unindividuated connection substitutes genuine emotional exchange for old parental behavior patterns. If you enter into such a relationship, your job is to be the absent parent for the demanding child. This means always subjugating your needs to the needs of the unindividuated other. The relationship works just as long as you are willing to fulfill your "parental" role.

Sounds awful, doesn't it? You'd surprised at how many of us create and participate in unindividuated connections. We are obsessive caregivers or perpetual victims in need of a caregiver. No matter which end of the relationship we fulfill, we substitute emotional honesty for an unindividuated connection.

THE ADDICTION CONNECTION

Much has been written about relationships among addicts, and much of it is very enlightening, so I only describe it briefly. Addictions in our culture are rampant. It seems everywhere you go, people are allowing themselves to become addicted to one substance or another. While most responsible writing on the subject does not consider addiction to a substance (such as alcohol, cocaine, etc.) the same as addiction to behavior (such sex, exercise, etc.), I include both in this description of the addiction connection because they fill the same need for the chronically discontent.

Joan has two of the most adorable Schnauzers you've ever seen. She's just crazy about those dogs. Over the past few years, she's immersed herself completely in the world of dog shows, where both of her dogs are decorated champions.

Since Joan has become involved in showing her dogs, she has lost all contact with her former friends. Everything in her life revolves around the dogs and shows. All her new friends are also deeply involved in the "dog world" and when they get together, it always has to do with dogs.

Joan spent a good deal of her life savings on a large motor home so that she could travel to the major dog shows across the country (she refuses to put her dogs on an airplane). Virtually every aspect of her life is centered on the dogs.

People like Joan create relationships around their addiction, whether it is alcohol, work, or even dog shows. They have discovered that they can create relationships that avoid emotional engagement by centering the relationships on a shared addiction. Both parties in an addiction connection are drawn together to support the ongoing demands of their common obsession. On the surface, these relationships appear to be strong and deeply felt, but when one party withdraws from the addiction, the relationship ultimately fails.

Alcoholics Anonymous has long championed the cause of those who wish to withdraw from addiction connections. AA recognizes that many relationships fall apart after the person no longer participates in the addiction and offers a ready-made group of new relationships through AA groups for addicts struggling to create a new life for themselves that is free from addictions.

Of course, even for people in recovery, there is a great temptation to substitute one addiction connection for another. For example, I remember working with one client who after becoming sober, delved deeply into a local evangelical church. He started attending services three and four times a week, and the only friends he made were from people who did the same. While he successfully overcame a potentially deadly addiction to alcohol, he continued to create addiction connections at church.

The addiction connection maintains at the core the addiction, not emotional exchange. All conversation revolves around the addiction. Without the addiction, there isn't any common ground for the relationship to thrive upon, and consequently, the connection quickly dies.

THE INTELLECTUAL CONNECTION

The last relationship that is common among the chronically discontent is the intellectual connection. This is a connection that is solely based on a common value or idea.

Tom is an investment banker. He loves to golf, collects good wine, and enjoys eating at great restaurants. Tom is extremely bright and has earned the respect of his colleagues and clients.

All of Tom's relationships are void of emotional involvement. While he is gregarious and talkative, he never talks about things that are truly personal. When his wife was rushed to the hospital with a ruptured appendix, Tom didn't tell anyone. Several of his golfing buddies found out about it through a mutual friend who works at the hospital and chided him for not telling them. Tom responded to their concern with "I didn't want to trouble you with it."

People like Tom who maintain intellectual connections use a variety of techniques to establish the agreement with others that emotional issues are off limits. For starters, they never discuss our true feelings. Sure, they say that they "love" the steak dinner a friend has grilled, that they "enjoyed" themselves at the party, but they never go beyond such surface matters. When others make the mistake of venturing into emotional territory, they use a variety of techniques to avoid it. In the example of Tom, he often would use a joke to lighten the situation and avoid an emotional discussion. Others sometimes just fall silent and then completely change the subject. Still others respond to an emotional exchange by posturing themselves as empathetic but without offering any of their own feelings to the discussion.

A client of mine who discovered he was HIV positive many years ago told his mother about his contracting the disease. His mother, clearly distraught by the information, never discussed it with him again. After a few years he felt it so odd, that he brought the subject up again, this time to tell her that he had been taking protease inhibitors (medication) that were working very well to suppress the virus in his body. She listened carefully and hugged him afterward, but still never brought the subject up again.

My client began to question his mother's love for him. "How could she not be curious about my health? Does she care about how I'm doing? Doesn't she know how grave this disease can be?" These and more questions kept him up at night.

My client's mother was undoubtedly deeply concerned about her son's health, but the threat of unbearable emotions kept her from being able to communicate her concern to her son. Any mention of HIV or AIDS caused her great distress, and she avoided it as much as possible.

The truth was that their relationship had been close, but only an intellectual connection for as long as my client could remember. They had never really shared their inner feelings, dreams, hopes, and fears with one another. Instead, they shared information about their interests and daily lives.

On the other hand, my client's life had been greatly affected by HIV, and now he truly wanted to share his life with his mother. With such a long history of no emotional honesty, neither one of them could break through the barrier to make the emotional exchange that both so wanted.

Walking Alone

The cocoon of emotional isolation that people with chronic discontent create for themselves makes them feel safe, yet it robs them of the joy of life. No matter how many people call us friend, we are slowly consumed inside by a slow hunger that isn't satisfied by our lighthearted conversations and kind gestures. We crave so much more, but are terrified to break through the wall we've built around our truest feelings. Until we find a way to keep emotionally honest relationships, we are trapped in the grip of our self-imposed isolation.

10

Remembered Feelings

(Are They Controlling Your Life?)

How do you know what if what you're feeling at this moment is the result of the here-and-now, a remembered feeling from the past, or a combination of both?

How do you know if what you feel for your new boyfriend is really connected to him or your memories of past relationships?

How do you know if your fear of starting a new business is legitimate caution or just old baggage from previous failures?

Can you trust your feelings?

The answer to this last question may surprise you. No, you can't trust your feelings—at least, not until you've developed your ability to sort out remembered feelings from primary feelings. This skill is critical to understanding and allowing your feelings to guide your life. Until you develop this emotional muscle, your feelings can be all over the map, and very unreliable.

You carry with you memories of every relationship you've ever known. What's downright scary about this fact is that you don't remember *exactly* every event, but a representation or what scientists sometimes call a "prototype" of the event. In other words, you're brain creates a synopsis of the relationship based on the salient feelings and critical events, and forgets everything in between. So when you recall that relationship, you remember only the highlights and your brain fills in the details with partial facts—and sometimes blatant fictions.

That's why from time to time you may say to your significant other: "Remember when we did such and such?" And he says to you with surprise in his voice, "We never did that!" What has happened is that one of your brains has created a fiction to fill in the holes of your memory. Consequently, the two of you don't remember the same event happening in the same way.

The reason this is important is that your emotional memory is faulty. You remember only strong feelings; the rest are typically forgotten. For example, you remember your childhood as very happy while your sister remembers nothing but arguments and discord. Or, your ex-wife remembers your marriage as being unhappy, while you remember it as mostly happy up until the last year.

Because remembered feelings can be faulty and are linked to the past and not the present moment, they can create havoc in your life. Until you're able to identify remembered feelings and distinguish them from primary feelings, you're in for some rough going. Only your primary feelings can guide your life toward happiness. These are the feelings that are connected to your present reality, and the ones that you want to listen to.

Sandy and Ralph are in their early '50s and have been married for over 25 years. They have raised two daughters, who are now both married and one is expecting their first grandchild. Shortly after the birth of their first child, Tina, Sandy suffered a severe bout of postpartum depression. For several years, she struggled with a deep and persistent depression that took her to the brink of suicide several times and ultimately resulted in an extended hospitalization. During those years, Ralph was forced to take on the full responsibility for the family, including hiring a nanny to care for young Tina.

After her hospitalization and 18 months of psychotherapy, Sandy's depression began to lift, and she gradually was able to function as a mother and wife again. After a few years, her recovery was complete and she was able to have a second child without incurring another depressive episode.

The years of Sandy's depression were very hard on Ralph. He grew accustomed to calling her several times a day to check on her and was always on alert for signs that her depression may have worsened. The day he had come home to find her on the kitchen floor after having taken an intentional overdose of medication was a memory that was seared into his mind, and he always feared that she might try to kill herself again.

After the birth of their second child, Sandy had returned to normal and was a very attentive and caring mother. She was deeply grateful for all that Ralph had done for her during her illness and loved him all the more for it.

Recently, however, Sandy had grown increasingly frustrated with Ralph. Now that the children were out of the house, she felt that distance between them had grown. More specifically, she felt that Ralph never opened up to her about his feelings. He was certainly kind and caring, but she had begun to wonder if she really knew him.

In couples counseling, Ralph confessed that he truly wanted to be more open with Sandy, but was always anxious about her ability to handle the unpleasantries of life. Over the years since her depression, he had continued to protect her from anything he felt might cause her to experience emotional stress. The result was that he had closed off a significant part of himself from the woman he loved so dearly.

Ralph's struggle was with his remembered feelings of an earlier time in his relationship with Sandy. Although both Sandy and Ralph readily admitted that Sandy hadn't experienced any symptoms of depression for almost two decades, the memory of his feelings about her depression were still strong. His present interactions with Sandy were strongly colored by those remembered feelings.

Here's another example. Rita's one big mistake in life was her first marriage. She was married at the age of 16 to a fast-driving, beer-drinking high school football player. A few months after they married, her husband began to come home from his night job drunk, and he would often abuse her verbally and physically. The night he slammed her against the refrigerator and broke her arm was the final straw, she left the mobile home where they lived and moved back with her parents. Two months later, she got a call from a state trooper that her husband had been driving drunk, driven off the road, flipped his convertible, and had been killed.

The trauma of that first marriage never left Rita. She eventually remarried, but now in her forties, she has great difficulty trusting men. Her current husband is, in her words, a "bore." He works as a draftsman by day and watches television most every evening. He doesn't like to go out much and has few friends. Their marriage is best described as cordial, but not intimate.

Although Rita is completely frustrated by her marriage, she can't imagine leaving it. "I've yet to meet a man who can keep his pants zipped up," she would say. In her mind, any man with "backbone" can't be trusted. So even though she isn't fulfilled by her marriage, she won't do anything about it.

Many of the important choices in Rita's life were determined by her remembered feelings from that first, disastrous marriage. The choice of her second husband, "a weak man with a good job," her resistance to making any big decisions (after all, the first big risk she took in life was, in her mind, a total failure), her deep mistrust of all men, and her inability to improve her current marriage all stem from those remembered feelings.

Rita settled for what she thought was safety, and in the process sacrificed her own happiness. The guilt and shame of that first marriage still haunted her and guided her life. She was determined to never feel such pain again, even if it meant diminishing her life to do it.

She refused to make herself vulnerable to anyone, much less a man. To be vulnerable flooded her with the pain of that first marriage, and she would always pull back. The memory of the past pain was great.

Each of us is deeply affected by our remembered feelings. The extent, however, to which we give those feelings control over our present lives is a choice we make. Our lives do not have to be determined by our past—unless we allow them to be.

The act of identifying and isolating the effect of remembered feelings is called *emotional discrimination*. What am I feeling right now? How much of this feeling is connected to my present circumstances? How much of it is connected to past experiences?

Learning to discriminate your feelings is part of building your emotional muscle. The first time you try it, it can be difficult to do. The more you do it, the easier it becomes. Eventually, emotional discrimination becomes a way of life.

Discrimination is a challenge for those of us with chronic discontent. We're not all accustomed or comfortable with examining our feelings. For the most part, we've suppressed our feelings, much less examined them.

Another challenge, once you've learned to discriminate your feelings, is to act "against" your remembered feelings. For example, the first time that Rita attempted to make herself vulnerable with her husband was excruciating difficult for her. Everything within her seemed to say that she was in danger. Pushing through that remembered feeling, and holding on to the primary feeling of the present eventually helped her to change her life and her marriage.

Feelings of ambivalence are almost always a strong sign of remembered feelings interfering with your primary feeling in the present moment. When you say to yourself, "I'm not really sure how I feel about this," it's an indication that your remembered feeling and your primary feeling are most likely at odds with each other.

For example, Susan really wanted to go back to work after her children were in school, but every time she came close to getting a job, she would retreat. Her primary feeling was that she wanted the autonomy and satisfaction of a career. Her remembered feeling was the constriction and drudgery she felt at the last job she held before becoming a mother. Intellectually she knew that not all jobs were like that, but the remembered feeling kept flooding back every time she'd get serious about starting work.

At first glance, Susan feels ambivalent about going to work. Some days she wants to, and other days she doesn't. As she sat with the feeling of ambivalence and examined it, she began to tease out the remembered feelings. The question for her was "Will I allow those remembered feelings to control me or will I branch out and try to begin a new career?" The choice was hers.

Susan chose to push through the feelings of ambivalence and act upon her primary feeling about wanting to have a career. Even though she felt vaguely uncomfortable, she made appointments, set up interviews, and ultimately accepted a job offer as a real estate assistant. Today, she has earned her real estate license and is satisfied with her new career.

The FEEL Process

To help you learn the process of discriminating your feelings, remember the acronym FEEL. FEEL is a simple, but very powerful tool.

FEEL is an acronym for:

Feel the feeling completely.
Examine the feeling
Express the feeling honestly
Let others *validate* your feelings

Feel the Feeling Completely

The first step in the FEEL process is to allow yourself to feel the feeling of the moment. Whatever that feeling is, you can heighten your sensitivity to it by naming it. In other words, ask yourself in the moment "What exactly am I feeling?" Force yourself to give it a name. Is it excitement, anxiety, sadness, fear? It's always helpful if you force yourself to give a specific name to your feeling.

Sue, who is single and very much wanting to meet a life partner, said that she often felt "revulsion" in the moment of withdrawal from those who were attempting to establish an intimate relationship with her. It never seemed to fail that when everything was going wonderfully and the other person seemed to be interested to taking the relationship to another level of commitment, she would find some fault about them (The Blemish Game described in Chapter 7) that she would then obsess on. She would so focus on this, that she said she would start to feel revulsion for the person and subsequently break it off.

The first step in the FEEL process is to allow yourself to embrace this feeling. Don't try to talk yourself out of it or belittle it. Feel it completely. If it is "revulsion" that you feel, as my friend did, then allow yourself to be repulsed. Don't try to change it or minimize it. Give the feeling a name.

Examine the Feeling

The next step in the FEEL process is to examine the feeling against the backdrop of current reality. What this means is that you ask yourself, "How much of this feeling is connected to what is actually happening to me?" Another way to reality test your feeling is to ask, "How would other people likely feel in this situation?"

The point of examining your feeling is not to belittle or condemn it, but to determine how much of your feeling is a primary feeling (the part of the feeling most connected to the present moment) how much is a remembered feeling from the past. If you're struggling with chronic discontent, then there is most likely an element of the remembered feeling of shame mixed in with other remembered feelings and primary feelings. At this step, you try your best to sort out the feelings.

When Sue feels revulsion, it is a combination of her primary feeling for the other person (which may actually be a positive feeling) and a strong, overpowering remembered feeling of shame. If the shame part of her feeling could speak, it would say things like: "Watch out! You're about to get entangled in a relationship that will evoke all kinds of feelings within you. Remember the last time you had a relationship? Remember how difficult and painful it was? Better get out of this now! You're doing just fine alone. It's better to be alone than in an emotional relationship."

Shame is insidious in the way that it invades your feelings. At this point in the process it is absolutely critical that you learn to recognize its effect on you and how you feel in any given moment.

The part of your feeling that is connected to the present reality is the primary feeling. This is the part of the feeling that is resulting from the here-and-now. This is the part of the feeling we want to honor and reinforce. The primary feeling is the feeling you want to hold on to.

Express the Feeling Honestly

After you've examined your feeling and extracted the primary feeling from the remembered feeling, the next crucial step is that you express the primary feeling honestly. If you feel angry, then you must express that anger constructively in the moment. If you feel attraction to the other person, you must express the attraction appropriately in the moment.

This can be extremely difficult step for CDers at first. We're not very practiced at demonstrating our feelings—in fact, we'd rather do anything *but* express how we feel.

Expression of the feeling in the moment that it occurs is important. Don't wait or try to express it in another form (such as sending an e-mail later in the day). Express the feeling immediately, for example with a hug or a frank discussion. Whatever the primary feeling is, force yourself to express it.

Notice that you express only the primary feeling and not the remembered feeling. The remembered feeling remains silent. For example, if your remembered feeling is a combination of shame and rejection, then choose not to give that feeling voice. By acknowledging, but not voicing, the remembered feeling, you disable it. A remembered feeling isn't relevant in the present moment and should be set aside.

The conflict between expressing the primary feeling and not expressing the remembered feeling can be very difficult. For example, when Sue feels revulsion but expresses affection for her date, it creates an internal struggle for her in that moment. The first time you attempt to do this, you will find it a struggle, too.

It is important that you push through your struggle and only express the primary feeling. No matter how powerful the remembered feeling is and how conflicted it makes you feel, force yourself to express only the primary feeling.

Sue discovered, as you will too, that pushing through the struggle actually gives you great clarity in your feelings. By allowing herself to express the affection, she soon found the remembered part of her feeling fading away. She was able to get past the "revulsion" and express her affection, which ultimately led her to a wonderful relationship.

Let Others Validate the Feeling

We need other people to acknowledge and respond to our feelings. For example, when you are in an argument with someone and he or she fails to acknowledge how he or she hurt you, it only makes you angrier. We crave emotional validation from our relationships. Perhaps the most satisfying aspect of emotions is having someone else validate them.

Validation is a critical guide to your behavior. For example, when you tell your boss that you are uncomfortable with your new project and he doesn't seem to understand or care, you just learned valuable information. You've discovered a disconnect in your relationship with your boss. Perhaps he isn't aware of how much work you already are doing. Perhaps he assumes that you have skills that you don't have. Whatever the disconnect might be, it informs your actions and is critical to effective behavior.

Emotional validation is very important to the maintenance of relationships. When your spouse rarely tells you that he loves you and you choose to ignore it, you may be headed for a troubled marriage. Likewise, by telling your spouse that you love her, and she validates your feeling by telling you that she loves you in return, you strengthen your relationship. Both of you can then go forward, confident in the strength of your marriage.

Sometimes in life, we express an emotion that others don't validate for us. For example, you tell your closest friend that you don't like another person that you've both just met. Your close friend tells you that she really likes this new person and disagrees with your feeling. As frustrating as it may be at times to have your feelings invalidated, they can help you to fine-tune your emotional life. Perhaps you're reacting to this person with a remembered feeling that wasn't apparent to you at the time? Perhaps your closest friend is reacting with a remembered feeling from her past? Whatever the case might be, it helps strength your emotional discrimination—a critical process for overcoming chronic discontent.

As we begin the next section of this book, you'll have plenty of opportunity to practice the FEEL process. Remember: feel it completely, express it honestly, examine it for reality, and let others validate the feeling. The more you practice this process, the better you'll become at understanding and listening to the intuitive wisdom of your feelings.

PART III

Living Richly:

5 Weeks to Feeling Better

Now we begin the journey that takes us deeper into your life and allows you to break free from chronic discontent. It's time to look at each of the four basic feelings, how you might be blocking each of the four feelings, and how you can enhance your experience of each one. Take your time as you read and work through the material. Stay with it—you'll emerge on the other side with a richer experience of life than you've known in a long time.

Remember, you can't feel better by just reading this book. You've got to experience it by doing the exercises. What do you have to lose? Aren't you ready to be done with chronic discontent?

Go ahead, make the commitment, and let's get down to work. . . .

How to Get Started

In this section of the book we will begin a program for helping
you deal with chronic discontent. It is a program that is carefully structured to create the kinds of experiences that lead to
lasting change, similar to the ones you might experience working with a professional psychotherapist. Although it is written in a format that you can complete alone, it is extremely
helpful to work through this program in conjunction with a
psychotherapist.

There are two commitments that you must now make if
you want to benefit from this program. First, you must commit
to reading and working through the entire program, without
skipping steps or jumping around. For maximal benefit, you
must work through the program sequentially from start to finish. It will take a commitment of around half an hour each
day—just about the same amount of time many of us take to
read the morning paper and have a cup of coffee.

The second commitment you must make is to read only the
material for a given day. Each day ends with a journaling
assignment, and the next day begins with a discussion what
you wrote on the previous day. The journaling becomes point-

less if you read ahead to the next day's discussion. Read only one day's material and then complete the journaling exercise for that same day. Then, put the book and your journal aside until the next day.

If you find yourself tempted, as I often am, to jump ahead and see what "the right answers are," then ask yourself why you are doing this. This program is about no one else but you. The only "right" answers are the answers that you give, and that honestly shed some insight into your own life. No other answer is correct. Reading ahead is a way of same as self-sabotaging your work. Resist the temptation.

If you are willing to make these two commitments, you're already on the road to making positive change. You will need to purchase a new notebook preferably filled with lined paper for writing. I personally prefer spiral notebooks, but any kind that you are comfortable with is fine. One quick note about privacy: Keep your notebook somewhere private. The work that you will accomplish is deeply personal and private, unless you choose to share it with others. Be sure that you keep your notebook somewhere where others won't be reading through it.

When you've got your notebook, turn the page and start the first day's exercise.

Week 1:

How Do You Withdraw?

In this week, we'll be looking at the ways in which we emotionally withdraw. As we've seen, emotional withdrawal is the core problem of chronic discontent around which all the other associated difficulties revolve. Each day this week, we'll tackle a different aspect of your emotional withdrawal.

Each day's program will consist of a short reading and a journal exercise. The short reading will focus on the previous day's journal exercise. To make this program work for you, it is important that you not read ahead. Do read only one day's program at a time.

Day 1: What You Didn't Say

The day we buried my grandfather is a day I'll never forget. We affectionately called him "Papa" and he was for all of us a figure that was bigger than life. Papa was a powerful man who had made a small fortune selling life insurance and in tree farming. Papa had his faults; he could be controlling, patriarchal, and demanding, but what I remember most was how much he loved us grandchildren. He took us fishing and taught us to drive his old Chevy station wagon out on the farm. For years, Papa was the president of the county board (in Louisiana it's called a "police jury"), and he loved to take his grandchildren with him to the county board meetings and let us watch the proceedings. Once, I even remember being the person who flipped the switch to turn on the Christmas lights downtown at the courthouse for the annual holiday celebration.

Toward the end of his life, Papa developed cancer of the larynx and had his vocal cords removed. After the surgery he learned to talk with one of those robotic sounding devices that he would hold to his throat (electrolarynx). I hated the sound of it, and what's more, the hole the surgery left in his throat terrified me (tracheotomy).

I didn't know how to deal with Papa's declining health, the strange noises he made with the electrolarynx, and the fact that he was dying. During those last years of Papa's life, I didn't visit him very often, and never went to see him the hospital.

His funeral was a very large affair. It seems that most of the town had known Papa, either from his later years in politics or his earlier years as a door-to-door life insurance salesman. The church was packed with mourners.

As my family and I rode in the limousine from the church to the cemetery, the finality of Papa suddenly hit me. He was gone, and I hadn't had the courage to tell him what he meant to me. All those fishing trips, fish fries, and afternoons of drinking Delaware Punch. Papa had been an enormous influence over my life, and I no longer had the chance to tell him how much I loved him.

As I think back on my grandfather, I'm grieved by the fact that I wasn't able to break through my own emotional wall and be there for him during those last years. My life would have been much less than it is today without him; how had I diminished his life by not being there for him?

TODAY'S JOURNAL EXERCISE

Think about the times in your life when you've wanted to tell someone important to you how you felt, but didn't. Maybe it scared you to be so vulnerable, or maybe you were like me and just waited until it was too late. What was it that you needed to say or do? What kept you from saying or doing it?

Day 2: Shaping Your Life

Start today by reading your journal exercise from yesterday.

As you read through what you've written, pay close attention to what you felt for the person and how you feel now having never expressed your feelings. We often excuse our behavior by telling ourselves "he (or she) knows how I feel, I just don't express it like other people." While there may be a crumb of truth in this, it is more of a statement of your tendency to withdraw from those who mean the most to you.

Give yourself a few moments to think about the effect of emotional withdrawal has had on this relationship. Is this what you want for your life? Is this the kind of relationship you want to have?

Here's what one man wrote after doing this exercise:

> The image that kept coming to mind was her hands. Those hands have raised our children, prepared thousands of meals, and kept a safe and loving home for all of us. I can't remember the last time I held those hands.

Years ago, when we first met, we would walk downtown to the theater holding hands. Honestly, I can't remember the last time I took her hand and walked down the street. What was the big deal? Why couldn't I bring myself to reach across the sofa at night while we were watching television and hold her hand? Why do I hit a wall when it comes to things like that? My wife and family mean everything to me; why can't I show them how much I love them.

Emotional withdrawal has had a profound shaping influence on your life. Every relationship in your life has been diminished by your emotional withdrawal, some more dramatically than others. Eventually the feelings get too threatening, and we pull back. Even though we may know that we love our spouse, children, friends, and parents, we are uncomfortable *feeling* it. Holding hands, saying "I love you," and hugging are just a few of things we avoid because they make us feel something. Only when the other person has initiated the gesture, do we respond.

Today's exercise is about acknowledging how your emotional withdrawal has affected all of your relationships throughout the entirety of your life. What you wrote about in yesterday's journal exercise is just a small sample of the large effect emotional withdrawal has had over your entire life. Virtually every relationship has been adversely affected by this withdrawal.

TODAY'S JOURNAL EXERCISE

Divide a journal page into four quadrants. Now, divide your life into quarters and give each one a label. If you're over 30, you might do it this way: child, teenager, early adult, adult. In each quadrant, write one of the labels. Now, within each quadrant, list the significant relationships of your life during that time. Leave enough space between the names to write a sentence or two about each.

Beside each name, write about how you emotionally withdrew from that relationship. For some relationships, you may have been more emotionally engaged than in others. Whatever the case, think about how you could have been more engaged, and write a sentence or two about it.

Day 3: Running Away from Trouble

Read yesterday's journal exercise.

Are you beginning to see a pattern? Do you see the imprint of emotional withdrawal on your life?

Many people this particular journal exercise moving, and maybe even upsetting. For most of us, there have been so many wasted opportunities to express our love and so many relationships that have been starved because of our inability to feed them. Who knew emotional withdrawal could have such a dramatic effect? Certainly we didn't.

Here's what one woman wrote after she completed this exercise:

> I've spent most of my life walking away from other people. I never realized it until now, but there it is, plain as day. I've turned my back on just about everyone. Some of them deserved it. Most of them didn't. I've always been jealous of Jean [a good friend] who still has most of her friends from childhood and college. I don't know

where most of mine are today. Why? I turned my back on every one of them. I don't know what the point of this exercise is, but I can see that I haven't been a very good friend.

The point of this exercise isn't to fill you with shame or sorrow. It's to show you how emotional withdrawal has shaped much of your life and experience. It isn't an easy thing to do, either.

The day I sat down and did it for the first time, I stayed awake all night afterward grieving over relationship after relationship that I had abandoned. So many people had been good to me, yet I had moved on without telling them how much they had meant to me and without being there for them when they needed me. I was overwhelmed with sorrow. After I moved through the sadness, one thing stuck in my mind: emotional withdrawal had deeply affected my life, and not for the better.

In today's journal exercise, we turn our attention to a more specific kind of emotional withdrawal: abandonment. For most of us, whenever a relationship fell into trouble, we walked away from it. We shut the door, and left all the pain behind—or so we thought.

TODAY'S JOURNAL EXERCISE

Make a list of all the relationships that have fallen into trouble and as a result, you abandoned rather than staying to work things out. Think carefully about this. Look back over your previous journal pages and reread what you've written in previous exercises. Make your list as complete as possible. Write a paragraph or two about the abandoned relationships that were the most painful.

Day 4: Burnt Bridges

Read yesterday's journal exercise.

Those of us with chronic discontent are likely to abandon rather than try to repair relationships troubles. When things relationships get a little rough, we walk away. The easiest thing to do at the time is to leave the troubles behind us.

To leave some relationships causes more emotional upheaval than staying, so in those we often make the choice to stay and emotionally withdraw. It might be a marriage or a business partnership, where leaving the other person would cause us to confront the other person and perhaps live through a difficult time of separation. The easiest escape from these kinds of relationships is to emotionally withdraw.

A special kind of emotional withdrawal is created by "carrying a grudge." Refusing to forgive another person gives you permission to retreat and a "legitimate" reason for your emotional withdrawal. By refusing to give up a grudge, you can safely maintain your emotional distance.

Take another look at what you wrote in the journal yesterday. How many relationships have you emotionally withdrawn from when physically leaving was too difficult? How many times have you persistently held a grudge to avoid painful feelings?

Consider what Irene wrote about her emotional withdrawal:

> I never forgave Tom for having an affair. I guess as I look back on it now, it was understandable. After our first son was born, I just wasn't interested in sex anymore and exhausted from having a newborn in the house. I would fall into bed and all I wanted was a few hours of sleep. Then came our second child six months later.

Within five years, I had had three children. The last thing on my mind was Tom and his needs.

He came to me and admitted the affair—I had no idea about it. I insisted that he get counseling, which he did, and since then he's been the model husband.

We never really talked about what really happened and I built a wall in my mind that I didn't want to cross. The truth is that I didn't just wall off the affair, I walled off part of myself, too. The idea of talking about what happened scared me to death, and I just didn't want to go there. Not with Tom. Not with anyone. I told no one about what had happened.

Ever since then Tom has done everything humanly possible to win me back, but I've always held him at arm's length. It seems like whenever I get close to letting go of it, the fear comes back. I can't really explain it. I lived so many years with this resentment that I don't know how to live without it.

Does Irene's story seem familiar to you? Is there someone in your life with whom you have unresolved issues? Do you feel frightened and ashamed whenever you think of bringing up these issues?

This is the essence of emotional withdrawal: hiding and avoiding the pain by not feeling anything in the relationship. Does this relationship mean something to you now? Do you want to be in a different place with this person?

TODAY'S JOURNAL EXERCISE

Today you write a letter to one person from whom you have emotionally withdrawn. This person can be living or not, but must be someone you care for and wish that things were/had been different. Don't worry—I'm not going to ask you to send this letter (unless, of course, you choose to). This letter is all about putting your feelings in one place where you can see them. Take plenty of time and describe what pain you might be avoiding, how you'd like to resolve things, and what this person means to you in the present.

Day 5—Day 7: Stretching Your Limits

Read the letter you wrote yesterday. You decide what to do with that letter. Maybe it stays in your journal as a marker of what you feel. Maybe it is a letter you want to send. Maybe it is the beginning of a conversation you need to start with someone. Whatever you do with this letter, it's your choice.

Here's a letter that a woman in her sixties wrote to her mother who had passed away a few years earlier:

Dear Mom,

I finally realized something today. I'm not proud of it. I wish it were different. I realized that I never really knew you.

All my life I felt as if I were a burden to you, one more thing to weigh down your life. I really didn't want to be a burden, so I tried to be invisible. I'm certain that you thought I was an ungrateful child. I wasn't. I just wanted you to love me the way that I wanted to be loved.

I know you loved me now that you're gone, but I didn't always feel that way. When I married Bob and we moved to California, I never dreamed that I would never move back home. Over the years you and I drifted apart. I can't even remember the last Christmas we spent together. That makes me very sad. You loved Christmas.

Somehow I always imagined that you didn't approve of me. I felt that you never really accepted Bob into the family and thought that I married beneath myself. You never said it, but I always felt that you disapproved of how I raised the children. When Sandy didn't go to college, I knew you thought I had failed.

As I look back, I can see that you really wanted the best for me. You and I saw things differently, but that was your way of showing love to me. In those last weeks in the hospital after your stroke, I didn't know what to say or do. It all seemed too awkward. Your life had gone by too fast. Then there wasn't any time left to make things better between us.

If I could do it differently, I know I would. I would show my love for you more often. I would have found a way to mend our differences. I miss you, Mom. Sometimes I hear your voice. Sometimes I see your face. If only we could sit down at your kitchen table and talk.

Why couldn't I break through it all and be there for you when you needed me? Why didn't we ever hug? Why couldn't I cry at your funeral? I miss you.

For most of us with chronic discontent, emotional withdrawal separates us from the people in our lives we want to be closest to. It's like a wall that we erect, and the longer that wall stands, the harder it becomes to tear it down. For many, an entire lifetime can pass before we realize the senselessness of that emotional wall.

What is the one thing that you feel comfortable doing that would chip away at the emotional walls that you've built in your relationships? What would stretch you to limit of your own comfort level while helping you to rebuild emotional contact with the people that mean the most to you?

In your journal, list three people that you've withdrawn from emotionally. For the next three days including today, make a plan to do something each day that breaks through the emotional wall. Maybe it's taking your son to an afternoon baseball game, taking your mother to lunch, or buying your business partner a beer after work. Whatever it is, make a plan that stretches you as far as your comfort level will allow.

There are three critical parts of this exercise—no matter what activity you do:

1. Be fully present and aware of the other person.
2. Plan to tell that person something about your feelings for them that you've never voiced before.
3. Listen and respond to the other person's feelings.

Afterward, take a moment sometime that day to write in your journal what you felt and what the other person felt during your time together.

I know this exercise is difficult. You can do this. You want to change your life? Go ahead, give this a try.

Week 2:

Getting Your Groove Back

Day 1: When Did You Last Feel Joy?

This week we begin tackling those intense feelings we've long avoided. The first of the four primary feelings we'll work with is joy.

TODAY'S JOURNAL EXERCISE

Think back to the last time you positively remember feelings joy. Write it in the form of story in your journal. Be sure to include as many details as you can remember. Take your time and imagine that you are writing this story for a popular magazine.

Day 2:

Read what you wrote for yesterday's journal exercise.

Here's my story of "last joy":

The house was at the end of Santa Fe's artsy Canyon Road. The galleries were all closed by the time we arrived for dinner at 6:30. I had made my one special dessert, a meringue layered cake that was a throwback to my childhood in Louisiana and Chef Shorty Leonard's favorite after-dinner delight. I loved that cake, which made my frustration all the greater when its delicate whipped cream icing started to slide off the cake and into my lap while we were still in the car. By the time I made it to the door, the icing was dripping on my shoes and the strawberries I had carefully sliced on top were leaving a trail on the dusty flagstone walkway.

The dinner was a special one. My good friend and fellow psychologist, Nesha, was celebrating her 37th birthday and all her close friends were gathered to mark the occasion. Nesha is a wonderful cook (before graduate school she had been the pastry chef at the prestigious Coyote Café), which made my disastrous dessert even more embarrassing.

As the evening went on, we all shared glasses of wine and a superb meal of Asian noodles and scallops. My dessert was appropriately served in bowls with spoons (I know Chef Shorty Leonard turned in his grave), but it tasted fine and seemed a good ending to a comforting evening with my favorite people. Little did I realize that what I would remember from that evening was far more than just the food.

At the table that evening were two psychologists (Nesha and myself), an interior designer to the Santa Fe wealthy-want-to-be-cowboys (David), an environmental attorney who was currently embroiled in a legal battle to save the silvery minnow in the Rio Grande (Steve), a teacher (Gayle), and a well-known writer of spiritual enlightenment and conscious dying (Joseph). Not your typical crowd, I suppose, but not at all unusual for Santa Fe, a geographic magnet for those of us who didn't quite fit the mold.

At the end of dessert, Nesha told us of a movie she had recently seen where a group of people were told after they died that they could only have one memory of their life on earth. What would the memory be?

The idea had moved Nesha. What one memory of her life was so outstanding, so wonderful, that she wished to carry it as the only reminder of life on earth?

As the conversation progressed, we moved around the table and each guest told of what memory they thought meant the most to them. Nesha said she wanted to carry the memory of her time in meditation, which of course, brought jeers from all of us. It just seemed too "spiritually correct" of an answer to be real. But she held firm—her time in meditation was the best experience of her life. I think she was telling the truth.

Around the table we went, each person telling their story of joy and ecstasy that they wished to carry into eternity. Then it came to me. What was my one treasured memory?

I fumbled. Surely there was something wonderful and joyous that I could take with me. But what was it? I began rewinding the tape of my life, frantically looking for something. Surely I wasn't so pathetic as to not have something I wanted to take from my time on earth. But what?

I said something about my days playing the piano in college, but I knew it wasn't the real answer. The question was burned into my brain. *When did I last feel something that I wanted to feel forever?*

For the days that followed, I was consumed with this question. What one memory was so wonderful that I would choose it above all others?

That question begged other important questions, too. What was it about a memory that made it so satisfying? What was the one thing I wanted to take from this life?

The quest for the answer had led me many places, even

before that fateful dinner. I realized that most of my life has been about answering the question, although I've been distracted, detoured, and avoided it for long stretches of time. What was the true nectar of my life?

As a psychologist who has worked in both clinical and corporate settings, I learned that the one thing that always led people into the dark territory of psychological anguish was the absence of joy. No client in therapy ever complained of feeling too much joy. No harried executive ever came to my office for relief from ecstasy.

Of this much I was certain—everyone craved joy, and the farther you move away from it, the harder it becomes to keep on living. Anxiety, depression, obsessive thinking, and self-destruction—they were all states of joylessness.

And now, sitting at a simple dinner party with friends, my finely tuned microscope was turned back on the reluctant scientist. Where was my joy?

Later that evening and into a sleepless night, it came to me; I remembered the last time I felt unencumbered joy. It was riding my bicycle home one winter evening when I was living in Key West, Florida five years earlier. I remember feeling the exhilaration as I felt the cool tropical breeze and watched the locals sitting on their front porches among mango and avocado trees. It was paradise.

In the years that had followed, I moved away from Key West to pursue "more important" career goals that I felt couldn't be fulfilled on a small island off the mainland of Florida. There were books to write, clients to see, and lectures to be given. It was important to me, so I thought, that I be important.

What I left behind in that simple island life was something that would become far more important to me than anything else: joy. It wasn't the place of Key West that was my joy; it was my life in that place. It was my experience. My life was simple, creative, and full of friends there. This brought me great joy.

Now? I had new friends and a career as both a struggling writer and psychologist. I lived in Santa Fe, one of the most beautiful spots on earth. But somehow, I had lost the joy. I had become more anxious, frustrated, and impatient. I wasn't the person I once was. Life had become increasingly more difficult, and I was getting less for the effort.

Nothing really made me feel content. Sure, there were good times and laughter, but they always quickly faded into a background of frustration and hard work. I was tired much of the time and found that I sometimes had to push myself to do things that I used to do with great pleasure.

So a simple parlor game question broke the dam. I had abandoned joy for lots of good and responsible reasons. But, there wasn't joy, so what was the point? Wasn't responsibility simply a tool for creating joy? Had I allowed the tail to wag the dog now?

What brought me joy wasn't the small bit of fame or success I had achieved. It may surprise you to know that it wasn't even that I had helped a few clients along the way, as important as that is to me. It was *simplicity*. A simple life brought me more joy than I can tell. A garden with tomatoes. A bicycle with a bell. A comfortable bed with big pillows. A loving spouse. Those things, together, filled me with joy.

TODAY'S JOURNAL EXERCISE

Once again, read your story of "last joy", but this time, read it with a critical eye. Pull the pieces of your story apart and analyze the parts. How long has it been since you last felt joy? What is it in your story that brings you joy? What can you boil your "joy" down to a few sentences?

Write a "review" of your story in your journal. Look for the themes and hidden meanings. What were you saying between the lines? What didn't you say? Is there some part of the story you didn't have the courage to put on paper?

Day 2: The Timeline of Joy

Joy is one of the great rewards of life. It is one of the four basic feelings, but it is by far the most important. Joy is the nectar we all want and crave. Where did you last know joy?

The most painful part of experiencing chronic discontent is the lack of joy. You didn't intend to give it up, it just happened. In fact, when you shut down the feeling side of yourself you did it because you thought it would protect joy, not leave it behind. But as you've seen, life doesn't work that way. You walk away from one feeling, and you walk away from them all.

When you suffer from chronic discontent, joy becomes a dirty word—a silly, childish emotion that has no place in your life. As joy fades into the distance of childhood, it becomes the sole property of children and Pollyannas who have deluded themselves into thinking that life was fun. You begin to believe that life isn't fun, and that anyone who acts as if it is, is crazy, stoned, or stupid. Life is serious business.

Still, in the back rooms of your heart and life, you crave joy. You roam your world looking for joy. Where is it? How can you feel it again? But you don't feel it, and you become ever more cynical. Maybe joy doesn't really exist? Maybe life is all about existential pain, thankless responsibility, and endless work? Maybe joy is something you leave behind in childhood, like teddy bears and the comfort of your mother's lap?

But you don't really believe any of that. Somewhere deep

inside you know that joy exists and that there must be something wrong with you when you can't seem to experience it anymore. Which, of course, makes you all the more frustrated when you are around others who seem to have joy. It only underscores your inability to feel.

To find out why you don't feel joy, we need to take a trip back in time to the place where you last remember feeling a strong sense of joy. For some, that trip will take you back to a very young age. For others, it may go back as far as your wedding day or the birth of a child. Whatever your last memory of joy is, let's take a visit to that place and time.

TODAY'S JOURNAL EXERCISE

To help you make this journey, I'd like for you to try this quick exercise. Get in a comfortable position and close your eyes if you like. Think back on all the good times in your life. As each memory pops into your head, write down a brief label for it, like: "met my husband," "my father came back from overseas," "birth of my daughter."

A note of caution: As you make your list, be very careful to list those events that were truly joyous and not events that *should* be joyous. For example, not all wedding days are filled with joy. If yours wasn't, don't list it. No one will see this list, so be honest. This is your life we're talking about—not the life you wish you had lived.

Take your time and make your list complete as possible. If it takes you a few hours or few days, do whatever it takes. Once you've completed the list, draw a line down a piece of paper, from top to bottom. This line is the timeline of your life, with the top being your birth and the bottom being right now. Take your list and distribute the events on this timeline. What do you see? At what time of life did you have the most joyous experiences? What was happening in your life during that time? What has changed in your life between then and now? Write about these things in your journal.

Day 3: The Triggers of Joy

Read what you wrote in yesterday's journal exercise.

There are two aspects of joy you need to know about. One is called a "trigger," and the other is called a "block." A trigger is an event that almost always precedes a feeling of joy. A block is an event that causes you to shut down a feeling.

Let's first take a look at what triggers joy for you. As I examined my list, I realized that joy was triggered when: 1) my life was simple and less stressful, and 2) I was able to express my creativity with little or no constraints. Almost every time I felt great joy, it was my experience of one of these two things that triggered it. (That's what I remembered about life in Key West.)

Here's what triggers joy for others:

- Martha, a Colorado housewife, remembers that her trigger for joy usually is abandonment in nature. For Martha, a long walk or camping trip in the mountains makes her feel ecstatic and wonderful.
- For John, the trigger is when he accomplishes something special, like the time he ran 60 yards to complete a touchdown in high school.

What are the triggers for your joy? Look over your list and meditate on this for a while. The triggers will become clear to you.

If you find that as you look over your list, you're having trouble identifying your trigger, try Nesha's dinner party exercise. Think of yourself as entering heaven after your own death. When you pass through the gates, you are told that you can only bring inside one joyous memory of your life on earth. All other memories will be left behind and forgotten for eternity. What memory will you take with you? What one memory was the highest point of your life? Now, examine that memory carefully. What made that experience happen for you? What was the trigger that created such joy?

TODAY'S JOURNAL EXERCISE

Write in your journal about your triggers for joy. Be creative and free associate (the first thing that comes to mind) without editing your thoughts. Write whatever comes to your mind when you pick up the pen and keep writing until you've exhausted your thoughts on triggers for joy. Don't worry if what you are writing seems silly or trivial. Write it all down.

Day 4: Facing the Block

Now comes the difficult part. When was the last time you experienced your trigger for joy? Not in quite some time, right? The problem is, every time you are in a situation to experience a trigger and the resulting joy, you pull back. You stop cold. You don't allow yourself to experience the trigger.

Why is this? It has something to do with the other important part of joy, your "block." You experienced some event, at some point in your life, that caused you great pain. For example, John, whose trigger was accomplishing something special, decided he really wanted to become a doctor and attempted to complete the pre-med requirements in college. John struggled through most of his college years and barely graduated with a C average, only to discover that no medical school would admit him. He was distraught, and for several years he floundered, not knowing what to do with his life. Finally, he settled on becoming a pharmaceutical salesman.

In John's mind, his trigger for joy had created a great deal of havoc and disappointment in his life. It was deeply painful for him—not only because he didn't reach his dream of medical school—but also because he decided that any pursuit of joy was likely to get the same results. So, like his father before him, he blocked his ability to feel joy.

The way John would block his joy is by never taking a risk. When the opportunity arose, he would chose the safe and easy path. Consequently, he never accomplished much out of the ordinary—and blocked his trigger to joy.

How are you blocking joy in your life? Is it:

- Filling your life with obligations so there's no time for joy?
- Creating a conflict whenever the possibility of joy arises?
- Taking an immediate, opposing action so that joy never happens?
- Convincing yourself that if something is joyful, it is automatically bad for you?

As you begin to think about your block to joy, many things will come to mind. You'll begin to see why it was necessary to shut down your feelings and how it was adaptive for you at the time. You'll also begin to experience the great cost of coping in this way. It's not uncommon to be overwhelmed with sadness over joyless years you've lived. Sit with sadness. Cry if you need to. Take a long walk and be with your grief. Talk to a trusted friend about it. Whatever you do, don't block the sadness now! It's OK to feel sad and to grieve over the loss of joy. You need to grieve over this.

How do you stop blocking joy? One proven method is by engaging in *incompatible behaviors*. Incompatible behaviors are those behaviors that are the behavioral opposite of your block. For example, if you block joy by avoiding risk, then you force yourself to do something that is a risk, like volunteering to sing solo in church. Incompatible behaviors prevent you from simultaneously blocking.

TODAY'S JOURNAL EXERCISE

What blocks do you normally use? Try to list at least three blocks that prevent you from experiencing joy. Beside each one write a short paragraph explaining how you use that block.

After you complete the above journaling activity, list an incompatible behavior for each block. Over the next few days, force yourself to perform at least one of your incompatible behaviors.

Day 5—Day 7: Practicing Joy

For one man who blocked his joy with work-related stress, he deliberately engaged a trigger by leaving the office during his lunch hour and visiting a local park. Here's what he wrote in his journal:

> Every day is the just about the same for me. The phone. The meetings. The lunches. More phone. More

e-mail. And then I do it all again. This is what I do every single day. There is no joy in this cubicle I call an office.

Today, instead of lunch, I walked by the water. The park was quiet and the birds were loud. I sat on the grass and stared at the water. I don't know how long it was, maybe ten minutes or so, before my shoulders began to relax and the stress of that place began to slide off me like toxic sludge. I began to feel alive again and remember that life isn't just work. This is life. It feels good. The sunshine, the water, the sound of children playing reminds me of my youth. Tomorrow I will come back and bring a book. When was the last time I read a book? Tomorrow I will lay here and read. It's good to feel alive in the middle of the day.

TODAY'S JOURNAL EXERCISE

For the next three days, choose to perform a trigger of joy each day. At the end of the day, write a paragraph or two in your journal about your experience.

Week 3:

What You Remember

Day 1: Remembering Pain

This week we will work with some of the remembered feelings that may be affecting your current relationships. Each journal exercise of this week is designed to help you recognize some of the emotional memories that you carry.

TODAY'S JOURNAL EXERCISE

What was the most painful experience of your life? If you were forced to rate all of your experiences according to trauma, which would earn the highest rating? Think about it carefully and make sure that you're choosing the one event that was most traumatic. As you write about this event in your journal, take extra care to be very specific about the details. What happened to you? Who was involved? How did it make you feel? How did it change your life?

Day 2: Remembering Childhood

Read yesterday's journal exercise.

The most powerful, shaping forces in our lives are our relationships. Some relationships have enormous impact on our lifelong decisions, while others have only a minimal effect.

What was the relationship that created the most painful experience of your life?

Janice wrote about her most painful experience:

I can't remember ever being paged at the office. It's rare that they page anyone over the loudspeaker, and especially someone like me. When I heard the page, I knew something must be wrong. I had no idea how wrong it was.

I called the operator and she asked me to go immediately to the human resources office. I remember thinking how strange it was. The only reason that they would do something like this is if I were being fired. When I walked into the office, I knew from the look on their faces that I was fired.

Human Resource people have never been my favorite people. They always seem to have smug smile and some trick up their sleeve. I guess they mean well, but I've never had a good experience with human resources. The human resource manager nervously asked me to sit down. I had met her only once and couldn't remember her name, so I smiled and sat down without saying anything.

The silence in the room was deafening. It seemed like minutes went by before she spoke, although I'm sure it was only seconds. She folded her hands on the desk and looked very serious. I knew I was so fired.

"There's been a very tragic situation," she said. "Janice I don't know how to tell you this." Another very long, deafening silence. "Your husband passed away this afternoon while he was in his office."

What? It didn't register at all. Am I fired? What is this woman saying to me? She doesn't even know me, much less my husband!

I don't remember much else of the conversation, except that it was very technical. Where his body was. What had happened. Who had called the company. Where I should go now. That was it.

Did I want someone to drive me home? No, I could drive myself. To say I was in shock is downplaying the whole thing. I was completely numb.

It wasn't until I pulled into the driveway that it really hit me. I saw his parents' car. They never came by without an invitation, now they were sitting in my living room. Oh my God. John's gone. . . .

I felt so cheated. I never got to say good-bye. We never got to have the life together we thought we would have. He was there that morning and then gone.

Since then, it's been very hard for me to trust anyone. I know he didn't do it intentionally, but I still find myself sometimes angry with him for leaving me like this. And then I get angry at myself for being angry at him.

I think I expect every relationship to die now. John was my closest friend and he died. I can't help it, I just expect people to leave me.

Janice's remembered feeling of abandonment by her husband's untimely death continued to affect her life until she was able to confront the feeling and acknowledge the effect it was having on her life.

In the case of Janice, it was a remembered feeling from adulthood that was a troubling influence. Many of us, including Janice, also have remembered feelings from our childhood. (As it turns out, Janice's father left her mother when she was only 13, so the remembered feeling of abandonment was jointly linked to her father and her husband.)

TODAY'S JOURNAL EXERCISE

Think back to your childhood and remember your caregivers (for most of us our caregivers were our parents). What remembered feelings are you carrying from your childhood relationship with your caregivers? Are those feelings still affecting your life? Are those feelings still affecting your relationship with your caregivers?

Day 3: Remembering Joy

Read yesterday's journal exercise.

As you think about what you wrote in yesterday's exercise, read what Thomas wrote:

> My mother is a very strong woman, and she raised all of us to be strong, too. She came from a generation of women that weren't supposed to have a career, so she focused all her energy on the family. As I look back on her now, I realize that she should have had a career of her own. I guess it just wasn't an option.
>
> The fact that mom focused so much of herself on

the family meant that she was involved in every decision regarding the children. She was determined that
we would all grow up the way she wanted us to. I hate to
say that she was manipulative, but it's really true. She
pushed us to do things her way, and when we got old
enough to say "no," she would try to manipulate us in
ways that she could control.

I remember her saying things like, "You don't want
to join the yearbook staff. It's just a lot of busy work."
When the truth was, she didn't want to be responsible
for taking me to all the after school meetings of the
yearbook staff. And that was just the tip of the iceberg.
God forbid that I date a girl she didn't approve of. She
knew better than to tell me not to date a girl (that
would have only made me more determined to do it), so
she'd take any opportunity to comment on the girl's
flaws. She'd do it in very subtle ways until we finally
broke it off. ("I wish she'd get a decent haircut." "Isn't
her father unemployed?" "Look at that girl, she's a
cheerleader. Why don't you ask her out? You don't have
to date only one girl . . .")

Even now, I am extremely sensitive to manipulation.
The minute I sense someone is trying to influence my
thinking, I immediately resist what they have to say.
When things go wrong, I sometimes imagine that I am
being manipulated in ways that turn out to not be true.
My remembered feelings of my mother's manipulations
still make me angry.

Thomas's emotional memory of his mother is still a force in
his life, despite an excellent education and years of professional
success. Coming to terms with these remembered feelings, as
Thomas did, is a big step toward disarming their influence in

your life. From this point on, Thomas can recognize when his anger at manipulation is merited by a situation and when it may be a holdover from his relationship with his mother.

It's also important to realize that not all remembered feelings are negative. Some are quite positive. For example, positive memories of your childhood summers in the mountains may influence you as an adult to return to the mountains often.

Although positive remembered feelings are pleasant, they still can cloud your perception of the current moment. As such, they prevent you from feeling what it is that you need to feel right now. To continue the previous example, perhaps your wife and children dread summer vacations because it means a week of boredom in the mountains? The pleasant remembered feelings from childhood may be blocking you from seeing what would really please everyone in your family.

TODAY'S JOURNAL EXERCISE

Take some time and remember the most joyous experience of your life. What was happening for you? What relationship was involved with the experience? How have you carried this remembered feeling forward to the present day?

Day 4: Today's Remembered Feelings

Read yesterday's journal exercise.

Here's what Carol, the mother of a newlywed, wrote:

> The day I got married was one of the happiest days of my life, so I couldn't believe that she didn't want a wedding. The elopement seemed like a slap in my face the day it happened. All I wanted was for her to be happy.

Now I can see that it wasn't about Tammy's happiness. It really was about what made me happy. What do I have to complain about? She's happily married to a wonderful man. It really is what I always wanted for her.

Remembered feelings of all types color your perception of the present moment. We function at our best when we acknowledge our remembered feelings and are careful about how we allow them to interfere with the present moment. Of course, there are times when remembered feelings are functional, such as the vague feeling of fear when you are in a dangerous situation that is similar to harmful situations you've experienced before. But even in these cases, you run the risk of "over-generalizing" the remembered feeling to situations that in reality aren't dangerous. For example, a remembered feeling from a painful or frightening encounter with a person of particular race or physical stature may generalize to all people of the same characteristic. The only way to effectively use remembered feelings is to feel, acknowledge, and examine them for appropriateness to the present moment.

TODAY'S JOURNAL EXERCISE

How have your remembered feelings influenced your behavior over the past 24 hours? Write about this in your journal.

Day 5: Make A Plan

Read yesterday's journal exercise.

Here's how one woman remembered being influenced by remembered feelings:

It's always driven me nuts when a spotlight turns green and the car ahead of me doesn't go. In just few seconds I can feel my blood pressure rise and I'm tempted to yell something nasty and include a choice piece of sign language. If they're on a cell phone, it drives me even crazier.

Yesterday on the way home from work it happened again. The car ahead of me had to be 20 years old and at least 20 feet long. The front seats were so tall, I couldn't see who was driving, but I imagine the driver must have been old. When the light turned green and the car didn't move, I did my little routine of honking and waving, but nothing happened. I waited until the traffic cleared and zipped on around, giving the driver my dirtiest look.

Then it hit me. I've been carrying around this remembered feeling of shame and humiliation for years from when my father would ridicule me for not doing something as efficiently as he would have done it. Dad was always so precise and perfect, and I was always silly and awkward.

Now I remember it—we were at the corner of old highway 7 and Jackson Street. I guess I didn't accelerate right when the light turned green, so Dad reached over and slammed the car into park, hopped out of the car, and then ran around to the driver's side, pushing me over to the passenger side. All the way as he drove home he berated me for not paying attention. He said I never paid attention to anything. He told me that if I didn't learn to pay attention, I'd be a failure in life.

I'm sure that's it. Or, at least, one instance from where it came from. Now, it's hard for me to be patient with other people's mistakes. My first reaction is to do the very thing I hated my Dad doing . . .

Remembered feelings often feel like knee-jerk reflexes, but you do have the power to stop before you act upon them. The first positive step is to recognize when you are acting on a remembered feeling. The second step is to make a plan on how to act the next time you feel that way.

TODAY'S JOURNAL EXERCISE

Read yesterday's journal exercise. Today, make a plan in your journal for how you will act the next time you encounter a situation that triggers that remembered feeling. Be specific in your plan on what you will force yourself to do and say. Make the plan realistic—something you will likely carry out.

Day 6: Practice Makes Perfect

Read yesterday's journal exercise.

Here's what the woman in yesterday's journal exercise wrote:

"Whenever I feel myself getting impatient with someone else's inefficiency, I will force myself to silently count to ten before doing or saying anything. Then, I will say something—anything—nice about that person. Then, if the situation truly merits it, I will offer helpful advice without ridicule or blame."

Making a plan for handling a remembered feeling at a time when you aren't consumed by that feeling helps you to act more appropriately to the present moment. When you're in the middle of the feeling, it's sometimes hard to pull back and examine what is happening. Making a plan and then attempting to keep it is a good way help yourself change.

The practice of identifying and examining remembered feelings helps you to become better at it. The more you do it, the easier it becomes. If you do it enough, it eventually becomes an automatic part of your behavior. As we've noted before, it is one of the most important skills of emotional well-being.

TODAY'S JOURNAL EXERCISE

Try to identify three or four ways in which you react based on a remembered feeling without including the one instance you've already written about. This can be difficult at first, but if you'll spend some time examining yourself, you'll easily come up with a list. Write about these in your journal.

Day 7: Good-Bye Letter

Read yesterday's journal exercise.

After a great deal of thought, one mother suddenly had an enormous insight into her remembered feelings. She realized that in dozens of ways she was raising her child just as her mother had raised her. Some of these remembered feelings had been a good influence on her parenting; others were not so good. She had never really looked at all the ways she reacted to her children from remembered feelings of her own childhood. For example, you should always fold the clothes as soon as they are finished drying. "Well, why?" she asked of herself. Can't the clothes wait if something more important is happening? Yet, she had also insisted, as had her mother, that the children fold the clothes immediately after the drier was finished and scolded them if they weren't. What good reason was there for this remembered feeling?

This journal exercise is an assignment that you must carry with you for the rest of your life. Feel and examine it. You must know how your past is influencing your feeling of the present moment.

TODAY'S JOURNAL EXERCISE

Today you will write a letter to the remembered feeling that has had the most influence in your life. Address the feeling as if it were a person. Tell the feeling how it has changed your life. Tell the feeling how you will always remember it, but refuse to let it run your life anymore.

Week 4:

Neutralizing the Shame

Shame is by far the most toxic of all the remembered feelings. Not only does it affect how you feel, it invades your most basic beliefs about life. Over time shame can actually change the way you view yourself and the world around you.

This week we will take a look at the shame-based beliefs that may be affecting your life. Each day this week, we will deal with a specific shame-based belief, explore the consequences, and challenge its validity in your life.

The following list contains many commonly held beliefs that usually originate from feelings of shame. Read the list and then rate each belief according to the following scale in box labeled "Rating" (leave the "Selected" box empty for now):

I have known myself to believe this to be true:

1	2	3	4	5
Never	Rarely	Occasionally	Often	Always

Rating	Belief	Selected
	1. If something bad has happened in my life, I am responsible.	
	2. My value is determined by how successful I am.	
	3. I am weak if I allow myself to be overcome with emotion.	
	4. It is very embarrassing to express emotion in public.	
	5. It is important that the people who love me approve of what I do.	
	6. I am a failure because I'm not powerful, successful, rich, etc.	
	7. Other people aren't interested in my problems.	
	8. There is almost always a self-serving, hidden reason for other people's actions.	
	9. If I allow other people to see my vulnerable side, they will inevitably use it against me.	
	10. Everyday life must be a struggle, and if it isn't, then I am doing something wrong, sinful, bad, etc.	

1	2	3	4	5
Never	Rarely	Occasionally	Often	Always

Rating	Belief	Selected
	11. I should never let my feelings interfere with my judgment.	
	12. Tomorrow will be better than today.	
	13. The best times in life come from escaping the everyday routine (e.g., vacations, parties, trips, etc.)	
	14. Friendships are a luxury in life.	
	15. If I don't get involved, then I can't get hurt.	
	16. If don't expect much, then I won't be disappointed.	
	17. Happiness can be bought.	
	18. Cheerful people usually aren't very smart.	

Once you have rated each statement, go back and select the seven statements that have the highest ratings. In the box labeled "Selected," place a check.

For each day this week, take one of the statements you selected and write about how that belief has influenced your life. Try to be as specific as possible, citing names, places, events, and times.

After you've don this, write about the events in your life that may have helped you adopt this shame-based belief. Think carefully about the influential events of your life, from childhood to the present and try to make a connection between this belief and an event in your life.

Here's what one man wrote about one of his shame-based beliefs:

When I read "If something bad has happened in my life, I am responsible," I knew I had to stop. That was it. That one belief has stuck with me all my life. I am responsible for everything bad that happens.

My father was a son of bitch. There, I said it. He was a mean, angry man. He had a real knack for zeroing in some perceived weakness and talking about it for days. It didn't matter what happened, he'd find something wrong, and then he'd pin the blame on me. It was always that way. I could never do anything right. Nothing I did was the way he would do it.

Last year when the systems crashed at the office, I was the one who spent a week without sleeping to fix it. It wasn't my problem. Hell, it was even my job. Something bad had happened, and I dove in head-first for the punishment.

The other night I heard on one of those television political dramas an actor say, "Every mistake doesn't involve carelessness." Really? I've always believed it did. If wasn't for all the careless, lazy, stupid, idiots in the world, everything would run perfectly.

How stupid is that? Bad things happen to good people. Sometimes I can't control everything. Just because things don't go according to plan doesn't mean that someone didn't do their job.

Week 5:

Building Emotionally Honest Relationships

Day 1: Getting It Right

This week we will begin to practice the steps of creating emotionally honest relationships. The steps aren't easy, but they will push you to create the kinds of relationships that are truly honest and fulfilling.

The first step in emotionally honest relationships is to clarify the facts. In other words, tell the truth about past and current events. Perhaps you're thinking that you've got this one already nailed, but think again. Sometimes, we omit details of our lives or deliberately "dress up" the unseemly parts to make them more palatable. And when you're trying to hide or disguise your true feelings, it's often tempting to change the facts. For example, when you didn't want to hurt your upset your husband by telling him how much you and children spent while shopping at the mall.

Most of us carry a great deal of shame about lying, yet we do it surprisingly often. Maybe we don't tell big lies, but we are constantly editing the stream of events to make them more acceptable to ourselves and those we love. It seems harmless—

in fact, Miss Manners would even suggest that it is civilized in certain situations—to edit what we tell other people. These distortions of the truth do far more damage than you might imagine. Much of the psychological stress you experience is because of mounting lies that you carry around.

I know these are strong words that may be hard to hear, but try to hear them without withdrawing. In fact, the more you may feel repulsed by what you are reading at this moment, the more it may be true for you.

For today's exercise, we will take one relationship and attempt to "clarify the facts." Although the exercise is for only one relationship, it is only a small start. Once you've done this exercise with one relationship, you should come back to this again and again for all the relationships that matter to you.

TODAY'S JOURNAL EXERCISE

Pick one important relationship in your life.

In your journal, write a list of all the facts of your life you've omitted or distorted in this relationship. Some may be small and insignificant ("I told my wife that I wasn't able to get a later flight when really I just wanted to arrive early enough to see the game on television") and some may be larger ("I never told him about the fling I had with our yoga teacher. After all, we were both single back then and if I told him he'd only get uptight and probably not want to take yoga classes anymore.").

Take your time. Make your list as complete as possible. If you aren't coming up with much, stretch this exercise over several days and take the time to think it over. If you do, you will amaze yourself at all the things you can list.

Day 2: Correcting the Errors

Read yesterday's journal exercise.

Here's what one woman wrote:

> I never told John about the abortion I had in college. It was such an awful time for me, and I guess I was afraid back then that he would think less of me for having had an abortion. I've always felt like there was a double standard between men and women. Why should I be looked down upon for making a mistake when a man can do the same thing, and it makes him more of a man?
>
> The truth is that I didn't tell him about the abortion and I should have. It will probably make my anxiety over my difficulty in becoming pregnant make sense to him. I've always thought that the abortion had something to do with my struggle to get pregnant. This is the first and most important item on my list.

The facts of our lives that we omit, edit, or misrepresent may seem harmless to our relationships. The truth is that they form an unseen barrier between you and the person with whom you want to develop an emotionally open relationship. Until you correct and clarify those facts, the barrier remains.

If you're like so many of us who struggled through this first stage of emotional honesty, you're thinking: "What good can come of me telling the truth now? It's over and done—buried in the past."

You've got to face this internal resistance and understand it for what it is—a barrier to emotional honesty. It's true that correcting old misstatements and omissions may create some difficulty in your relationship. The truth is that until you do your best to correct intentional dishonesty, you aren't being completely honest, no matter how good-intentioned you may be.

Make a plan to begin correcting the items on your list from yesterday's exercise. Start with an easy item on the list, and plan to correct it first. Don't attempt to correct all the items at one time—it may be too much for the other person to handle. Plan to take your time and do it in a comfortable way. Make sure that you include in the plan plenty of time to talk through the issues.

Day 3: True Feelings

Don't move on to today's reading until you've had a chance to follow through with your plan in yesterday's assignment. When you've corrected most of the items on the list, you're ready to read today's material.

A step beyond insisting on complete honesty of the facts is to reveal the truth about your thoughts and feelings. It's one thing to be honest about objective events, and quite another thing entirely to own your true feelings. This step can feel very threatening, but it is essential to creating the kinds of relationships you crave.

Most often we are dishonest about our feelings because we want to "spare" the other person's feelings, or so we tell ourselves. The truth is, when we swallow our feelings it is most often ourselves we are trying to protect. How so? Admitting feelings that aren't expected by the other person requires us to be vulnerable. For example, telling your boyfriend that you love him when you imagine that he doesn't share the feeling makes you feel very vulnerable. Instead of owning the feeling, you hide it and act as if you really don't love care that much for him. Likewise, when you disagree with another person but refuse to show it, you are protecting yourself from the discomfort of a disagreement. In the moment, it may seem easier to just avoid the unpleasantness of a disagreement, so you swallow your feelings.

The problem with hiding your feelings is that it always seems as if it is just about to work, but never does. You think you will avoid a disagreement by not showing your feelings, but it only makes matters worse down the road when your feelings eventually spill out or you withdraw from the relationship.

Fulfilling relationships are based directly on your willingness and ability to express your feelings *as you feel them*. Pleasant, unpleasant, vulnerable, or safe—whatever the feeling creates, you must be willing to go there.

TODAY'S JOURNAL EXERCISE

Using the same relationship as the previous exercises this week, think about feelings you had in recent memory that you didn't express. Write about those feelings and why you imagined you couldn't express them in the relationship.

Day 4: Difficult Feelings

Read yesterday's journal exercise.

What feelings are you swallowing? Examples of what others have written include:

"I really hate it when he tells off-color jokes when we're with our friends, but I laugh at them anyway."

"It really makes me uncomfortable when I see her talking on her cell phone while driving the kids to school."

"It makes me feel really wonderful when he holds my hand. I wish he'd do it more often."

Whatever the feeling is, expressing it is the key to an emotionally honest relationship. It isn't easy to do, especially if you haven't had much practice with expressing difficult feelings, but the payoff can be truly rewarding. Learning to express your feelings in a way that respects the other person is crucial. After all, if you express what you're feeling, you must be prepared to allow the other person to express what they feel, too.

This step can be a powerful trigger for emotional shame, so be on the watch for it. If you find yourself feeling guilty for having expressed your feelings, or apologizing for your feelings, then you've triggered some of the old shame that has held you back. Remember: the best way to handle shame is to acknowledge it and then push beyond it.

TODAY'S JOURNAL EXERCISE

Today you will practice expressing difficult feelings. In your journal, describe a recent situation where you weren't able to express a difficult feeling. After describing it, write a scenario where you do express your difficult feeling. Imagine yourself in the situation and how the other person might react. Write every detail of the interaction as you see it in your mind.

Day 5: Nondefensiveness

One of the important skills of expressing difficult feelings is that of learning to allow others to have their own feelings without shame or remorse. For example, one man described the situation of telling his parents that he didn't like the way they treated his new wife. He told them he felt that they were judgmental and condescending to her. When he told his parents this, his mother began to cry. It was excruciatingly difficult for him not to apologize for his feelings. She went on and on about how hard she had tried to be friendly with his wife, but the wife seemed to be unresponsive. "How can you blame me for her coldness?" the mother sobbed.

This man's mother had a right to her feelings, even if those feelings didn't validate what he told her. She, too, needs to express her experience of the situation. Emotionally honest relationships allow both parties to express their feelings without judgment or condemnation. Allowing this free exchange of feelings is the goal.

The important lesson here is that expressing your feelings doesn't necessarily mean that others will validate those feelings. When they don't, you shouldn't try to manipulate or force them to validate your feelings. Simply allow the differing perspectives to coexist.

TODAY'S JOURNAL EXERCISE

Imagine expressing the most difficult feeling in your relationship. Now, imagine that after you've expressed your feeling, the other person has the completely opposite feeling of yours. Finally, imagine that you aren't defensive or angry at the other person's response. Instead, you allow them to have their feelings without judgment or condemnation. Write about this imagined scenario in your journal.

Day 6: Empathy

Read yesterday's journal exercise.

Here's what one woman (I'll call her Beth) wrote about her encounter with her husband who had left her for another, younger woman:

Craig left about 30 minutes ago. He arrived at 2 this afternoon and stayed until 8:30. I knew when he walked in the door that he was ready to talk. I asked him right off the bat if I could give him a hug. He said "yes" and we hugged for what seemed like a few minutes. Then we sat down and really talked for the first time since he left.

We both cried—a lot. I told him everything I was feeling, including about all the resentment and anger I had toward him. I told him I was actually glad that he had left because it made me see the truth about our relationship and myself. I said that I couldn't believe that I had put up with so much and that was a very hard thing to admit. I think of myself as a strong woman and not the type to put up with a man treating her badly. And now I had to admit that I had been doing it for years.

He told me that he still loved me and had been overcome with grief over our separation for the past few weeks. He said that he walked the floor at night remembering me in every room of the house. He apologized for how he had treated me. I could tell that he meant every word, and it felt good to hear.

It was the hardest thing I've ever done, telling him how much he hurt me. I am certain that he came to the house wanting to get back together, but I had to say what I felt. I know he was shocked to hear it from me, because I'd never said any of it before. I'd dreamed he would come back, and now that he wanted to, it felt like I was pushing him away. But I wasn't. For the first time since we married, I was letting him see the real part of me.

Now that he's gone, I feel so light and free. I know that Craig isn't evil, just really hurt and scared. I also know that I can live without him. Let me say that another way: I have chosen to live without him. Now that feels really good. For the first time in months I feel like I can move forward and start living my life again. Funny how telling him the truth really did set me free.

What Beth discovered is what we all discover through these exercises: emotional honesty is liberating and exhilarating. It's a freedom that defies words.

On the other side of emotional honesty is a deep empathy for the feelings of others. Once you are free to express what you feel, you are also free to feel what others are feeling. It's an amazing experience, and you'll never understand it until you experience it. Beth wasn't able to really feel what Craig was experiencing until she was honest with him about her own feelings. When she was finally honest, it was like a wall came down and the two of them touched each other in a way they had never done before.

Empathy is a skill of emotional honesty. Understanding and experiencing the feelings of others is critical to relationships. You're not free to completely feel another person's feelings until you've allowed your own true feelings to show.

One tool for increasing your skill of empathy is to attempt to see the "inner child" in another person. For today's exercise, practice seeing the inner child in the other person. Write a description of that child: what he or she wants, needs, loves, hates, and fears.

Day 7: The Fiction of You

Read yesterday's journal exercise.

Beth wrote the following in her journal about her soon-to-be ex-husband Craig:

> I can see in Craig a young boy, about 9 or 10 years old, riding his bike as fast as he can down the street. He loves excitement and speed. He hates school. He never does his homework. He loves a good adventure and is always out and about looking for some trouble to get into.
>
> He wants his father to love him, but all he ever gets are shouts and spankings. He wants his mother to love him, but she's much too proper to love a little boy in the way he understands love.
>
> He sees himself as a failure at school. He's not much better at sports, but he tries. The other boys like him and laugh at his jokes. They like to go down by the pond with him and smoke cigarettes and look at the *Playboy* he stole from under his father's mattress.
>
> If he had any success, it was with the girls. They seemed to like him and he always had at least one following him around. He learned really young that his

strongest asset was his appeal to girls. It helped him feel like he wasn't such a failure after all.

Beth was able to see in Craig the inner child who was fun-loving and irresponsible. She saw how much he wanted love, but was never really able to get it from the people who mattered. Even as a child, he expected to disappoint those who loved him.

The kind of empathy that Beth has achieved is critical to her future relationships. As she learns to see the inner child in those around her, she begins to open the door wide for emotional exchange.

The final step in creating emotionally honest relationships is exposing the *fiction of your* story. What this means is reaching the place where you no longer try to sell your relationships on your competence and success. How you present yourself in relationships becomes more about the here-and-now than it is about your story.

Let me explain this with an example from my own profession. In the mental health field, there are varying levels of education and licensure. Some professionals have earned a master's degree (M.A. or M.S.W.) and others have earned doctorates (Ph.D.) and still others have earned medical degrees (M.D.). The honest truth, however, is that regardless of the level of education, there are plenty of highly educated psychotherapists who aren't very good, and some of lower education who are extremely talented and experienced.

Our degrees are our stories. They say nothing about who we are in the present moment. They say nothing about our ability to help people. When I have achieved this level of emotionally honesty, I can admit this. Even though I've earned a Ph.D., I can admit that there are psychotherapists with far less education who are better than I am. I can admit that I don't have a clue as to how to treat some clients. I can admit that I really just don't like some clients. I can admit that some clients bore me to death.

This level of honesty is about putting aside my story of being a highly trained psychologist and admitting the truth about me as a person. It's about putting aside the sham that each of us carries and owning the harsh reality of ourselves.

When I sit down with another psychotherapist who presents the professional façade of "I can treat anything," I'm immediately put off. None of us can treat everything perfectly. That's the truth of the here-and-now. The fiction of our stories is that we are trained to do it all, and it's just that: fiction. All of us have professional doubts and insecurities, and no amount of training will change that.

TODAY'S JOURNAL EXERCISE

What is your story? Your racket? The "sham" that you present to the world? How do you attempt to make yourself appear competent and confident in all ways? Write the fiction of you in your journal.

THE ROAD AHEAD

You've finished the program. Take the time to celebrate this milestone. More importantly, take the time to look back and remember all that you've learned. What you've learned in these fives weeks shouldn't stop here. Keep practicing the skills you've learned. From time to time, revisit your journal. Reread old passages and continue writing on issues that come to mind. You've made some major steps in changing your life, so don't stop now.

A Note to Psychotherapists: Treating Clients with Chronic Discontent

Dysthymia is undoubtedly the most widely occurring and, surprisingly, least understood of all the psychopathologies. Generally, it is understood by mental health professionals to be a low level, persistent form of depression. In other words, most have considered dysthymia to be simply an early phase of clinical depression, and consequently, the psychotherapeutic treatment strategies they offer follow the same course as major depression. Although these strategies haven't worked as well as they do with major depression, the lack of efficacy has generally been attributed to the "chronic" nature of dysthymia and not to the ineffectiveness of treatment.

There is, however, a growing recognition among clinicians and researchers alike, that while dysthymia is related to depression, the effective treatment strategy is different than those used for major depression. In other words, there is evidence that the successful psychotherapeutic treatment of dysthymia is distinctly different those of other forms of depression.

Psychotherapy & Dysthymia

Until recent times, clinicians believed that dysthymia (described as "chronic depression") didn't respond well to psychotherapy.[1] There is, in fact, considerable data to support this viewpoint.[2]

Most all published studies to date have used some variety of Beck's cognitive behavioral therapy (CBT) model for treating dysthymia. For the past twenty years, CBT has generally has been recognized as one of the most effective psychotherapeutic treatments for depression, and hence it was thought to be appropriate for dysthymia, as well.

In short, the CBT model requires the therapist to identify the automatic thoughts and underlying beliefs associated with negative feelings. The therapist then sets out to expose the errors of logic and irrational nature of the underlying beliefs and argue against them.

In the landmark book, *Cognitive Therapy of Depression*, Beck et al write:

"The therapist can use a variety of arguments and exercises to help patients examine the validity of self-defeating beliefs. Patients do not change their beliefs because of the number of counterarguments, but rather because particular arguments make sense to them."[3]

Examples of the kinds of self-defeating beliefs a therapist might challenge include:

- "Because I am a good person, I deserve to succeed in life and fate will make sure that good things happen to me."
- "Because I have not done as well as I could, I deserve to suffer."

These self-defeating beliefs often surface quickly with the severely depressed client, but not necessarily with dysthymic clients. These clients may or may not hold many of the typical self-defeating beliefs, and furthermore, challenging the beliefs they do hold doesn't generally result in lasting results. While Beck's model works well with the severely depressed, its efficacy doesn't hold up with dysthymia.

A study of the effects of Beck's CBT on 62 dysthymic males after 16 weeks of treatment with CBT showed limited success.[4] The authors of this study concluded "chronically depressed patients had slower and less complete responses to CBT . . ." Another recent study published in *The American Journal of Psychiatry*, concludes that for dysthymic patients: "cognitive behavior therapy had no effect on clinical symptoms."[5]

Medication Isn't the Cure, Either

With the publication of several well-known books and numerous periodical articles on the utility of the new antidepressants on treating depression, many mental health practitioners assumed that these medications would also effectively treat dysthymia. A careful review of the medical research in this area, however, simply doesn't support this view. To date there are is little evidence to suggest that medication alone is effective in the treatment of dysthymia. Positive outcomes in the treatment of dysthymia with pharmacotherapy in almost all reports occurs when medication is combined with psychotherapy that contains some element of interpersonal communication and relationship assistance.

Furthermore, dysthymic clients are also far less likely to respond positively to antidepressant medication than are more severely depressed clients. For example, in a double-blind randomized trial of (an SSRI marketed as Zoloft) and imipramine (an antidepressant marketed as Tofranil), 635 chronically depressed clients were treated.[6] The study was sponsored by Pfizer Pharmaceuticals and recruited subjects from throughout the United States. After 12 weeks of treatment with either medication (more than sufficient time for the medication to have an effect), only 17% achieved full recovery, while 35% reported only a partial response, and 48% reported no response at all.

At the National Institute of Mental Health, a large-scale study of depression (Treatment of Depression Collaborative Research Project) found that even with all levels of depression (major and chronic depression included together), psychotherapy was equally as effective in treating depression as was medication (Imipramine). Furthermore, one of the psychotherapies tested which showed positive outcomes was interpersonal psychotherapy.

A recent article published in the *Journal of the American Medical Association* notes that: "Recent literature syntheses concluded that there is insufficient evidence to recommend pharmacotherapy for minor depression."[7]

Both research and clinical experience with dysthymia suggests that traditional methods medication and/or psychotherapy for treating major depression are not as effective in treating dysthymia. Given the large number of clients with dysthymia, psychotherapists are faced with the question: What is the most effective treatment for dysthymia?

Treating Dysthymia

The answer to these questions seems to come from much of the past theory and recent research on emotion and interpersonal relationships. To start, let's briefly consider some of the theoretical beginnings that lead us to more current developments in the treatment of dysthymia.

Early in pioneers in psychological research noted that those who suffered from chronic anxieties and depression (often labeled "neurotics") showed a marked inability to identify their feelings. Karen Horney, a psychoanalyst and contemporary of Freud's, wrote in 1945:

"For him [the neurotic] awareness of feelings and desires is at a low ebb. Often the only feelings experienced consciously and clearly are reactions of fear and anger to blows dealt to vulnerable spots. And even these may be repressed."[8]

Horney departed from Freud's inner-conflict theories by suggesting that "neuroses are generated by disturbances in human relationships."[9] The suggestion that psychological difficulties were, at least, in part due to faulty human relations was radical for the time and sparked a new school of thought within the relatively narrow confines of psychoanalysis and the larger field of psychology. Along with other pioneers like Alfred Adler and Eric Fromm, the interpersonal links of psychopathology began to take hold.

In the 1960s, Sidney Jourard was a leading force in the field of humanistic psychology, serving as the president for the Association for Humanistic Psychology. Until his untimely death in 1974, he researched and published a large volume of research on the importance of self-disclosure and interpersonal relationships on mental health. In brief, he believed an unhealthy personality is someone who has not truly made himself known to at least one other human being, and therefore does not know himself. In his best-known book, *The Transparent Self*, he writes:

"We camouflage our true being before others to protect ourselves against criticism or rejection. This protection comes at a steep price. When we are not truly known by the other people in our lives, we are misunderstood. When we are misunderstood, especially by family and friends, we join the 'lonely crowd.' Worse, when we succeed in hiding our being from others, we tend to loose touch with our real selves. This loss of self contributes to illness in its myriad forms."[10]

In more recent times, researchers have tackled the link between interpersonal relationships and chronic depression from an empirical standpoint. Literally hundreds of studies have examined these issues, and recently several excellent literature reviews have been published attempting to summarize what is known. In the journal *Psychiatry*, T.J. Scheff published a comprehensive review of the current research and concluded that depression is inexorably linked with the breakdown of social bonds. Further, Scheff noted that this breakdown is often precipitated by intense feelings of shame.[11]

It is out of this line of research that the key to treating dysthymia is emerging. Briefly, that model is:

- Each of us has a mortal need for relationships that allow for the open and honest expression of our feelings, and for those feelings to be validated by another human being. *The degree to which dysthymia begins to emerge in our lives is directly related to our ability to create and maintain a network of emotionally honest relationships.*
- Given this theoretical premise, we can arrive at two important conclusions about dysthymia and its treatment:
  - First, one must be able to identify, control, and express his or her emotions clearly and honestly.
  - Secondly, one must be capable of staying emotionally engaged within a relationship (maintain strong social bonds).

If either one of these conditions are not met for an extended period of time, the likely result is the onset of dysthymia. Likewise, treating clients with dysthymia requires identifying the blocks to these two conditions and helping the client to overcome them. Let's take a closer look at each of these conditions and how they contribute to onset and maintenance of dysthymia.

ONE MUST BE ABLE TO IDENTIFY, CONTROL, AND EXPRESS HIS OR HER EMOTIONS CLEARLY AND HONESTLY.

In this first condition, honest expression of emotion, there are several potential problems that may arise:

- Biological factors, including problems with neurotransmitters, cause the client to have an abnormally high threshold for feeling pleasant emotions.
- Shame-based experiences in early life taught one to effectively avoid situations and thoughts that evoke emotions.

When biological factors are the problem, current antidepressant medications including the selective serotonin reuptake inhibitors (SSRIs) can be of great help. Diagnosing a biological cause to dysthymia is difficult and often can only be conclusively done by placing a client on medication and observing the results. For this reason, a psychopharmacologist should be consulted for clients who may require medication. While a discussion of psychopharmacology is beyond the scope of this chapter, it is important to note that a review of the most successful treatment for all forms of depression utilizes both psychotherapy and medication (Wright & Thase, 1992). The authors conclude: "the overall results of these studies suggest that, when effective, both cognitive therapy and pharmacotherapy appear to produce changes across response dimensions." (p. 452)[12]

For most dysthymic clients, shame, in all its myriad forms, is the essence of the problem. Shame around the experience and/or expression of emotion causes the client to emotionally withdraw from relationships. The shell of the relationship remains, but the richness emotional content is eviscerated. This results in the client "going through the motions" of relationships but not experiencing the satisfaction and fulfillment that only emotionally engaged relationships can provide.

ONE MUST BE CAPABLE OF STAYING EMOTIONALLY ENGAGED WITHIN A RELATIONSHIP.

When emotional avoidance is the problem (as it most always is), then therapy must tackle the task to extinguishing the avoidance response. In other words, the conditioned avoidance of emotions must be broken by causing the client to be progressively exposed to his or her feelings.

As for the second condition, staying emotionally engaged in a relationship, the primary problem associated with the onset of dysthymia is withdrawal. Clients with dysthymia almost always describe repeated marriage failures, broken friendships, and troubled relationships at work. At the core of these broken relationships is one of two kinds of withdrawal: either the client has physically withdrawn from the relationship, for example, by moving out of the house or quitting a job, or has emotionally withdrawn by disguising, hiding, or misrepresenting feelings.

These two conditions, (1) honest expression of emotion and (2) maintaining ongoing emotionally engaged in relationships, must always be the central focus of treating the client with dysthymia.

With Our Noses Pressed to the Glass

One of the most surprising findings of a recent survey of more than 2,000 mental health professionals is that more than 35% report that they personally struggle or have struggled with ongoing, chronic depression.

Why would this be so? Mostly, because we are trained to be acute observers of behavior. As such, we are tempted to live on the sidelines, watching the action of life go by. Rather than feeling the richness of life's ups and downs, we are busy classifying, diagnosing, and treating it. It is all too easy for us to become "armchair human beings" who are experts in a subject that we don't actually participate in ourselves. Emotionally, it is precisely this approach to life that creates dysthymia.

When a psychotherapist sees the world through a lens colored with dysthymia, it is only natural that he or she fails to see it in clients. When dysthymia is the norm, other people with dysthymia seem normal, too.

This might explain, in part, why the diagnostic rates of dysthymia differ greatly between psychotherapists in the United States and the rest of the world. For example, recent epidemiological study in Canada showed the incidence rate of dysthymia to be 3–5% higher than those reported in the United States. Similar discrepancies exist with European epidemiological data. Because mental health professionals in these countries are generally more aware of dysthymia and its pervasive symptoms, it is diagnosed more frequently than in the United States where the experience dysthymia is more widely accepted as "normal" among educated professionals.

I believe, as do many mental health professionals, that the effective psychotherapist must first look inward at himself or herself prior to treating clients. Given the high rate of dysthymia among psychotherapists, it seems critical that any psychotherapist wanting to use the program in this book with clients should first work through it themselves. Only when you can begin to see life without dysthymia can you be attuned and empathetic to the subtle manifestations of it in your clients.

How to Use this Book with Clients

This book has been designed to be used as a stand-alone self-help aid or as a workbook for use in psychotherapy. The first three sections of the book provide a solid background for the dysthymic client beginning psychotherapy. I'd recommend that the client read those sections during the first weeks of therapy, and come to sessions prepared to talk about what they've read.

The fourth section is a self-guided program of journaling that spans five weeks. This section shouldn't be read until you and the client are ready to begin working on the root causes of the dysthymia. Each day of the week presents a new challenge to the client, and some may prefer to take the work more slowly. Encourage the client to take the exercises at their own pace, and bring their journal to each session.

The journaling exercises are intended to help the client self-identify problematic issues. Allow the client to talk about whatever is significant for him or her from those exercises. Each client is different, and some will respond more powerfully than others to certain exercises. The client's journal should be a springboard from which each therapy session begins.

You will find that a few dysthymic clients may be resistant to doing the journaling exercises. I'd recommend using this resistance as a place to start in therapy. Why is the journaling a problem? What does the client fear? How can the two of you take the journey together through the exercises?

Most often confronting the resistance and working through it is enough to get the client started on the journaling. In the rare cases where it isn't, then it can be helpful to identify with the client the issues that are interfering with his or her active participation in therapy.

A client who refuses to actively participate in therapy may have a vested interest in not getting better. Explorations of "What is the payoff for not participating?" and "What is the benefit of keeping your chronic discontent (dysthymia)?" can sometimes move the client forward. Finally, a review of why the client sought therapy, the objectives of therapy, and the requirement of active participation may be in order.

1. Akiskal, H. S., Rosenthal, T. L., Haykal, R. F., Lemmi, H., Rosenthal, R. H., & Scott-Strauss, A. (1980). "Characterological depressions: Clinical and sleep EEG findings separating 'subaffective dysthymias' from 'character spectrum disorders.'" *Archives of General Psychiatry, 37,* 777–783.
   Keller, M. B. (1990). "Diagnostic and course-of-illness variables pertinent to refractory depression." In A. Tasman, S. M. Goldfinger, & C. A. Kaufman (Eds.), *Review of Psychiatry* (Vol. 9, pp. 10–32). Washington, DC.: American Psychiatric Press.
2. Keller, M. B., & Shapiro, R. W. (1982). "Double depression: Superimposition of acute depressive episodes on chronic depressive disorders." *American Journal of Psychiatry, 139,* 438–442.

Keller, M. B. & Shapiro, R. W. (1984). "Double depression, major depression, and dysthymia: Distinct entities or different phases of a single disorder?" *Psychopharmacology Bulletin*, *20*, 399–402.

Keller, M. B., Lavori, P. W., Endicott, J., Coryell, W., & Klerman, G. (1983). "Double depression: A two-year follow-up." *American Journal of Psychiatry*, *140*, 680–694.

Keller, M. B., Lavori, P. W., Lewis, C. E., & Klerman, G. (1983). "Predictors of relapse in major depressive disorder." *Journal of the American Medical Association*, *250*, 3299–3304.

3. Beck, A. T., Rush, A. J., Shaw, B. F., & Emery, G. (1979). *Cognitive Therapy of Depression*. New York: Guilford Press.

4. Thase, M. E. (1992). "Long-term treatments of recurrent depressive disorders." *Journal of Clinical Psychiatry*, *53*, 32–44.

Thase, M. E., Reynolds, C. F., Frank, E., Simmons, A.D., Garamoni, G. D., McGeary, J., Harden, T., Fasiczka, A. L., & Cahalane, J. F. (1994). "Response to cognitive-behavioral therapy in chronic depression." *Psychiatry Research*, *3*, 204–214.

5. Ravindran, A. V., Anisman, H., Merali, Z., Charbonneau, Y., et. al., (1999). "Treatment of dysthymia with group cognitive therapy and pharmacotherapy: Clinical symptoms and functional impairments." *The American Journal of Psychiatry*, *156*, 1608–1617.

6. Keller, M. B., et. al., (1998). "The treatment of chronic depression: Part 2. A double-blind, randomized trial of sertraline and Imipramine." *Journal of Clinical Psychiatry*, *59*, 598–607.

7. Williams, J.W., Barrett, J., Oxman, T., Frank, E., et. al. (2000). "Treatment of dysthymia and minor depression in primary care: A randomized controlled trial in older adults." *The Journal of the American Medical Association*, *284*, 1519–1526.

8. Homey, K. (1945). *Our Inner Conflicts: A Constructive Theory of Neurosis*. New York: W.W. Norton, p. 27.

9. Homey, K. (1945). *Our Inner Conflicts: A Constructive Theory of Neurosis*. New York: W.W. Norton, p. 12.

10. Jourard, Sidney M. (1971). *The Transparent Self*. New York: Van Nostrand Reinhold Company, p. vii–viii.

11. Scheff, T. J. (2001). "Shame and community: Social components in depression." *Psychiatry*, *64*, 202–214.

12. Wright, J. H. & Thase, M. E. (1992). "Cognitive and biological therapies: A synthesis." *Psychiatric Annals*, *22*, 451–458.

INDEX